EVERYMAN, I will go with thee,

and be thy guide,

In thy most need to go by thy side

ARISTOTLE

Born at Stageira in 384 B.C. Studied at the
Academy, 367–347, and spent the next three
years at the court of Hermeias in Assos. He then
moved to Mitylene in Lesbos and taught there
until 343, when he became tutor to Alexander.
After the latter's accession to the throne of Mace-
donia in 336, Aristotle returned to Athens and
founded the Lyceum. He fled to Chalcis in
Euboea following Alexander's death in 323, and
died there in 322.

DEMETRIUS AND LONGINUS

Otherwise unknown Greek rhetoricians most
probably of the first century A.D.

Aristotle's Poetics
Demetrius on Style
Longinus on the Sublime

INTRODUCTION BY
JOHN WARRINGTON

DENT: LONDON
EVERYMAN'S LIBRARY
DUTTON: NEW YORK

© *Introduction and translation of Aristotle's 'Poetics',*
J. M. Dent & Sons Ltd, 1963

Made in Great Britain
at the
Aldine Press · Letchworth · Herts
for

J. M. DENT & SONS LTD
Aldine House · Bedford Street · London
First included in Everyman's Library 1963
Last reprinted 1969

NO. *901*

SBN: 460 00901 x

INTRODUCTION

THIS volume contains three of the most famous specimens of ancient Greek literary criticism. Aristotle's *Poetics* is today the most widely read of all his works. It was originally the first book of a summary of lectures on the art of poetry, dealing with both tragedy and epic; a second book, now lost, was devoted to comedy.

Most, if not all, of the Stagirite's works show great inequalities of writing, passages of wonderful lucidity and polish being followed by others in a style so abrupt and crabbed as to tax the ingenuity of his interpreters, both ancient and modern. This phenomenon is particularly noticeable in the *Poetics*: the beginning is quite satisfactory, but as the work proceeds one observes a certain neglect of form, and the exposition is reduced at times to something little more than a succession of notes. A translator is therefore obliged to make more than ordinary use of paraphrase, rearrangement or expansion of sentences and so forth, because space forbids a running commentary and a plethora of explanatory footnotes is undesirable. The form of the Greek text, which necessitates a fairly free translation, is due, I believe, to several facts which, though by no means certain, seem to be indicated by internal evidence. The first and third books of Aristotle's *Rhetoric* contain three explicit references to the *Poetics*, while the latter (1456ª35) refers once to the *Rhetoric* This suggests that Aristotle, having completed his lec tures on the epic and dramatic arts, proceeded to the subject of rhetoric *before* committing the *Poetics* to writing; that he undertook this latter task at a considerably later date, possibly in a hurry and when the lectures were no longer fresh in his memory, so that he was compelled to rely largely upon old notes; and that the resulting text was never revised.

This would also help to explain certain anomalies and informalities which the reader will no doubt detect even in translation. Such are (a) the anticipatory use of technical terms, e.g. 'simple plot', whose definitions are deferred; (b) inconsistencies of thought, as when we are told in one place that the personages of tragedy are 'above our own level' and in another that they are 'like ourselves'; (c) lapses of memory, e.g. misquotations from Homer and even from the author's own earlier remarks.

These defects, however, are slight when compared with the achievement as a whole. Aristotle declares in the final pages of his *Nicomachean Ethics* that the highest state of human perfection is the contemplation of eternal truth, and he believes that the man who knows most is likely to live best. He does not, like Socrates, identify virtue and knowledge, but he does consider accurate knowledge of whatever kind an aid to right living. This practical purpose which underlies all his teaching becomes crystal clear in his treatment of poetry. His summary of the lectures on poetry was intended for the use of men who had heard him and who would therefore not be unduly inconvenienced by the absence of literary form. It was intended, in fact, as a manual of instruction. Aristotle tells his pupils what to seek and what to avoid in constructing a poetic drama; what is the aim of such a drama; how the fulfilment of that aim establishes the form of the drama; by what means that aim is fulfilled and by what errors an author may fall short of its fulfilment; what are the charges brought by critics against poets, and how they may be refuted.

But the practical purpose of the *Poetics* has also a moral aspect more important to an educated Athenian than any mere critical theory of literature. Plato, in the tenth book of the *Republic*, frowns upon the poet's ability to stir the muddy waters of emotion, an ability which is exercised more than in any other way in the art of tragic poetry. Aristotle, on the contrary, as a more acute observer of human nature, knows that emotion must have an outlet or purge (*catharsis*) if it is not to burst the banks of self-control and rationality. It finds this outlet in the 'pity and fear' stimulated by tragedy and producing the pleasure of vicarious experience. It is true that too much of such experience must prove harmful; but the Athenians could witness tragedies only at the annual festivals of Dionysus.

It is likewise true, as Gilbert Murray said, that 'if any young writer took this book as a manual of rules by which to "commence poet", he would find himself embarrassed'. The work, however, should be read not as a dogmatic textbook, but as a first attempt by one who was perhaps the greatest genius of all time to establish a rational order in one sector of the field of creative art, as he had already done in almost every domain of contemporary knowledge.

A modern reader may be puzzled by Aristotle's doctrine of the tragic hero, by his insistence upon plot as more important than character, and by his extraordinarily 'soulless' handling of literary style. Yet if we recall the conventions of the Athenian stage; if we consider Aristotle's view of the purpose of tragedy and the means thereto; and if we take account of his inductive method and his analysis of poetic diction, his shortcomings in these respects (if such they really are) will be recognized as excusable because at any rate logical.

Lessing spoke nonsense when he referred to the *Poetics*

as 'infallible as the *Elements* of Euclid'. But Saintsbury, the historian of criticism, is indubitably right when he assures us that 'it is impossible for anyone who undertakes the office of a critic to omit the study of Aristotle without very grave harm'; for Aristotle reveals the fundamental principles of dramatic art, which no critic and no dramatist can ignore without falling headlong into irrelevance and ineptitude.

The other members of this volume are works by otherwise unknown Greek rhetoricians, most probably of the first century A.D. The treatise by Demetrius, *On Style*,[1] translated here by T. A. Moxon, owes much both to Aristotle and to Theophrastus. It discusses first the construction of sentences, and then four types of style in Greek prose—stately, polished, plain and powerful. The value of this work depends less on the theories it propounds than on the practical test of the principles of good taste which it provides. One of the most pleasing features of Demetrius is his constant appeal to and quotation from the great Greek authors.

The more famous treatise *On the Sublime* was for long attributed to Longinus of Emesa (*c.* A.D. 213–73), the friend and minister of Zenobia, Queen of Palmyra. Since this attribution has been proved false, the author is commonly called Pseudo-Longinus in modern books of reference. The work, printed here in H. L. Havell's well-known translation, is acknowledged as one of the great masterpieces of literary criticism. Written, apparently, to supplement an earlier treatise of the same title by Caecilius of Calacte, it shows a close connection with Tacitus and Quintilian. Longinus is far removed from Aristotle. He considered the sublime language of great literature as 'the true ring of a great soul', and he was

[1] *Peri Hermēneias.* The word means rather 'rhetorical expression'.

echoed long afterwards by Cardinal Newman, who proclaimed style to be 'the shadow of a personality'—two observations that would have seemed to Aristotle, the ancestor of all academic dons, nothing better than downright sentimentality. Longinus defines the sublime in literature as an excellence and supremacy in language whose aim is to dumbfound the audience by simultaneous deployment of all the speaker's power. He goes on to discuss the success of classical Greek poetry and prose, from Homer to Demosthenes, in attaining the sublime, quoting also *Genesis* and Cicero; and he concludes with some remarks on the relation of literature to society.

The present translation of Aristotle's *Poetics*, made specially for this volume in Everyman's Library, is based upon the great edition of Ingram Bywater (1898). The numbered and lettered sections, as well as their titles, are mine. Bekker numbers are placed within square brackets in the text. I have removed two sections (1452^b14–27 and 1456^b20–57^a30) and placed them as appendices in the belief that they are interpolated fragments. A few shorter parentheses which complicate or interrupt the flow of thought are treated as footnotes—a device which Aristotle would no doubt have used if it had been invented in his time. All such footnotes are followed by (A.); the remainder are mine.

Wherever it was necessary to retain Greek words and phrases I have transliterated them for the benefit of readers unacquainted with the Greek alphabet. This was not done by Moxon and Havell in their respective versions of Demetrius and Longinus; but I have not felt entitled, when preparing the volume, to alter their texts. Accordingly I have transliterated such passages in an appendix (page 57). I have also prepared an index of authors and artists covering all three works. This not only gives page references, but also, wherever possible, identifies the person, concerned and supplies their dates.

JOHN WARRINGTON.

1963.

THE FOLLOWING WORKS OF ARISTOTLE
ARE IN EVERYMAN'S LIBRARY:

Metaphysics (No. 1000)
Ethics (No. 547)
Politics and Athenian Constitution (No. 605)
Poetics, with Demetrius *On Style*
   and Longinus *On the Sublime* (No. 901)
Prior and Posterior Analytics (No. 450)

BIBLIOGRAPHICAL NOTE

THE most important editions of Aristotle's *Poetics* are those of G. Morel, 1555; I. Bekker in his standard edition of Aristotle's Works, 1831; J. Vahlen, 1867; I. Bywater, 1898 (with commentary, 1909); S. H. Butcher, 1902; D. S. Margoliouth, 1911; A. Rostagni, 1927.

Demetrius was edited by L. Radermacher, 1901. The definitive text is that of W. Rhys Roberts, with Introduction, notes, glossary and bibliography, 1902. Rhys Roberts was also responsible for the best edition of Longinus, 1899; 2nd ed., 1909.

See S. H. Butcher, *Aristotle's Theory of Poetry and Fine Arts*, 1902; J. T. Sheppard, *Greek Tragedy*, 1920; L. Cooper, *The Poetics of Aristotle, its Meaning and Influence*, 1924; A. W. Pickard-Cambridge, *Dithyramb, Tragedy and Comedy*, 1927; F. L. Lucas, *Tragedy in Relation to Aristotle's Poetics*, 1930; J. W. H. Atkins, *Literary Criticism in Antiquity*, 1934; T. S. Eliot, *The Use of Poetry and the Use of Criticism in Antiquity*, 1934; T. R. Henn, *Longinus and English Criticism*, 1934; J. Jones, *On Aristotle and Greek Tragedy*, 1962; E. Olson (ed.), *Aristotle's Poetics and English Literature*, 1966. For mythological persons and events see *Everyman's Classical Dictionary*, 1961.

CONTENTS

xiii

CONTENTS

ARISTOTLE'S POETICS

TRANSLATED BY JOHN WARRINGTON

I. INTRODUCTORY: DEFINITION AND
SPECIES OF POETRY

[1447ᵃ] Our subject is Poetry, and I propose to speak not only of the art in general, but also of its species [1] and their respective capacities; of the construction of plot necessary for the making of a good poem; of the number and nature of a poem's constituent parts; and of other such relevant matters. Let us follow the natural order, beginning with the primary facts.

Epic poetry and Tragedy, as also Comedy, Dithyrambic poetry, and most flute-playing and lyre-playing, are all, taken as a whole, modes of imitation. But they differ from one another in three ways, either (*A*) by a difference of kind in their means, or (*B*) by differences in their objects, or (*C*) in the manner of their imitations.

(*A*) Just as some, whether by art or constant practice, use form and colour in order to imitate and portray many things, while others use the voice, so also in the above-mentioned arts the means employed as a whole are rhythm, language, and harmony—used, however, either singly or in certain combinations. A combination of rhythm and harmony alone is the means in flute-playing, lyre-playing, and any other arts there may be of the same description, e.g. imitative piping. Rhythm alone, without harmony, is the means in a dancer's imitations; yes, even a dancer may employ rhythmic movement to represent men's characters, as well as what they do and suffer.

---

[1] Epic, Tragedy, and Comedy. Lyric poetry was so closely linked with musical accompaniment that Aristotle presumably considered it as belonging to the art of *melopoea*, i.e. the art of music-making.

There is further an art which imitates by language alone, without harmony, in prose or in verse, and if the latter, either [1447^b] in some one or in a plurality of metres. This form of imitation is to this day without a name.[1] We have no common name for a mime of Sophron or Xenarchus and a Socratic dialogue;[2] and we would still be without one even if the imitation in each case were in iambics, elegiacs or some other kind of verse. What people do, of course, is to place the word 'poet' after the name of the metre, and talk of 'elegiac poets' and 'epic poets,' thinking that they call them poets not on account of the imitative nature of their work, but indiscriminately on account of the metre in which they write. Even those who write in verse on medicine or physics are usually described in this way; yet Homer and Empedocles have nothing in common except their metre; so the right thing is to call one of them a poet, and the other should be described as a physicist rather than a poet. The same principle would hold good, too, if the imitation in these instances were in *all* metres, like Chaeremon's rhapsody *The Centaur*; and Chaeremon one is obliged to recognize as a poet. So much, then, for these arts. Finally there are certain other arts—e.g. Dithyramb and Nomic poetry,[3] Tragedy, and Comedy—which employ every one of the means enumerated, viz. rhythm, melody, and verse; with this difference, however, that these three kinds of means are in some of them all used together, and in others introduced separately one after another. These

---

[1] We call it 'literature', for which the Greeks had no word.

[2] The mime, a humorous representation of the scenes and personalities of everyday life, was the nearest approach of the Greeks to what we should call prose fiction. Some have maintained that Sophron's mimes suggested the dialogue form to Plato, and one of them is thought to be reproduced in verse in the XVth Idyll of Theocritus.

[3] The nome was a solo hymn accompanied by the lyre.

elements of difference in the above arts I describe as the 'means of imitation.'

(B) [1448ᵃ] The objects represented by an imitator are actions performed by men who are necessarily either good or bad.[1] Consequently the agents represented must be either above our own level of goodness, or beneath it, or exactly such as we ourselves are; in the same way as, among painters, the personages of Polygnotus are above the ordinary level of nature, those of Pauson below it, and those of Dionysius faithful likenesses.[2] It is clear that each of the above-mentioned arts will admit of these differences, and that it will become a separate art by representing objects that differ in this respect. Even in dancing, flute-playing, and lyre-playing such diversities are possible; and they are also possible in the nameless art that employs language, prose, or verse without harmony, as its means. Homer's personages, for example, are more exalted than we are; Cleophon's are just like ourselves; while those of Hegemon of Thasos, the inventor of parody,[3] and Nicochares, author of the *Deiliad*, are beneath our level. The same is true of the Dithyramb and the Nome: the personages may be represented in them with the difference exemplified in the ... of ...[4] and Argas, and in the *Cyclopses* of Timotheus and Philoxenus. Tragedy and Comedy, moreover, are distinguished in the same way; the aim of Comedy is to exhibit men as worse, and of Tragedy as better, than those of the present day.

[1] The varieties of human character almost always derive from this distinction, since the line between virtue and vice is one that divides the whole of mankind.—(A.)

[2] Dr Hamilton Fyfe illustrates Aristotle's meaning here by suggesting Gainsborough, Hogarth, and 'any portrait painter who makes what are called good likenesses' as respective modern parallels to Polygnotus, Pauson, and Dionysius.

[3] i.e. as a special form of poetical literature.

[4] Lacunae in the text.

(*C*) A third difference in these arts lies in the manner in which each kind of object is represented. Given both the same means and the same kind of object for imitation, a poet may either (1) speak at one moment in narrative and at another in an assumed character, as Homer does; or (2) he may remain the same throughout, without any such change; or (3) his imitation may take the form of representing the whole story dramatically and his personages as actually doing the things described.

As we remarked at the outset, therefore, the differences in the imitation performed by these arts come under three heads: their means, their objects, and their manner.

Sophocles then, as an imitator, ranks in one respect with Homer, for both portray high-souled men; but in another he is to be classed with Aristophanes, because both present their personages as acting and doing. This is in fact, according to some, why plays are called dramas (things performed), because the personages act the story. Hence too the Dorians pose as the inventors of both Tragedy and Comedy. The Megarians in Greece put forward this claim as regards Comedy, on the ground that it arose when Megara became a democracy;[1] and so do the Megarians in Sicily,[2] arguing that the poet Epicharmus flourished a good deal earlier than Chionides and Magnes.[3] Tragedy too is claimed by some of the Dorians in Peloponnesus, who argue from the very words 'comedy' and 'drama'. In pointing out that the Doric word for outlying hamlets is *kōmai*, which the Athenians call *dēmoi*, they assume that comedians got their name not from *kōmazein* (to revel), but from their strolling from one *kōmē* to another before they were appreciated

[1] *c.* 600 B.C.
[2] The citizens of Megara Hyblaea.
[3] Assumed by Aristotle to have been the earliest comic poets at Athens (*c.* 500–450 B.C.).

in the city. They also observe that the Doric word for 'to act' is *dran*, [1448^b] whereas the Athenians use *prattein*.

So much then for the number and nature of the points of difference in the imitation performed by these arts.

II. The Origin of Dramatic Poetry

The general origin of poetry is evidently due to two causes, each of them part and parcel of human nature. (1) *Imitation* is natural to man from childhood upwards. One of the things that make him superior to brute beasts is the fact that he is the most imitative of all animals, and begins to learn by way of imitation; and it is moreover natural for all human beings to delight in works of imitation. Experience demonstrates the truth of this latter point: though the objects themselves may be offensive to sight, we enjoy viewing the most realistic representations of them in art, e.g. the forms of the lowest animals, dead bodies, etc. The explanation is as follows. To be learning something is the greatest of pleasures not only to philosophers but also to the rest of mankind, even though the latter have only a limited capacity for it. The reason for the pleasure derived from looking at pictures is that one is at the same time learning —gathering the meaning of things, e.g. that the man there is so-and-so; for if one has never before seen the object represented, one's pleasure will not arise from the picture as an imitation of it, but from the workmanship, the colouring, or some such cause. Imitation then, being natural to us, as also is (2) *the sense of harmony and rhythm* (the metres being obviously species of rhythm), it was through their original aptitude and by successive improvements, for the most part gradual, on their initial efforts that certain men created poetry out of their improvisations.

Poetry, however, soon branched out into two kinds according to the differences of character in the individual poets. The graver among them would represent noble

8

actions and those of noble personages, and the meaner sort the actions of the ignoble. The latter class began by composing invectives, just as the former produced hymns and panegyrics. We have no such works by any of the pre-Homeric poets, though there were probably many such writers among them; but it is possible to cite examples from Homer onwards, e.g. his *Margites*,[1] and similar poems by other hands. An iambic metre was introduced as the most appropriate to this poetry of invective; hence our use of the word 'iambic', because it was the metre of their 'iambs' or invectives against one another. Consequently some of the old poets became writers of heroic and others of iambic verse. Homer, however, occupies a unique position: just as he was the poet *par excellence* in the serious style, standing alone not only through the literary excellence but also through the dramatic character of his imitations, so also he was the first to outline for us the general forms of Comedy by substituting ridicule for invective and giving it a dramatic cast; his *Margites* in fact bears the same relation to modern comedies as do the *Iliad* [1449ᵃ] and *Odyssey* to modern tragedies. But as soon as Tragedy and Comedy came upon the scene, those who had a natural tendency to one style of poetry became writers of comedies instead of iambs, and those with a natural bent for the other style became writers of tragedies rather than of epics, because these new forms of art were grander and of higher esteem than the old.

To consider and decide, both theoretically and in relation to the theatre, whether Tragedy is now all that it need be in its formative elements does not belong to our present inquiry.

It is certain that Tragedy and Comedy both began in

---

[1] A lost work. It was the mock-heroic story of a rich fool who 'knew many works but knew them all imperfectly'.

improvisations; the former originated with the authors of the Dithyramb, the latter with those of the phallic songs which still survive as institutions in many cities. The subsequent advance of Tragedy was gradual, through successive improvements upon whatever the poets found to hand at each stage. It was indeed only after a long process of modification that the development of Tragedy came to a halt on attaining to its natural form. (1) The number of actors was first increased from one to two by Aeschylus, who also curtailed the function of the Chorus and made the spoken passages the principal part of the play. (2) Sophocles added a third actor and introduced scenery. (3) Tragedy acquired also its present length and solemn character. Discarding short stories and a ludicrous diction as it emerged from its satyric stage, it assumed, though only at a late point in its progress, a tone of dignity; and its metre changed then from trochaic to iambic. The original use of the trochaic tetrameter was due to the fact that early dramatic verse was satyric and more closely connected with dancing than it is today. As soon, however, as a spoken part was introduced, nature herself discovered the appropriate metre. The iambic is, of course, the most speakable of metres, as appears from the fact that we very often fall into it in conversation, whereas we seldom talk in hexameters, and then only when we depart from the usual tone of speech. (4) Another modification was a plurality of episodes. As for other matters—the additional embellishments [1] and the account of their introduction—these must be passed over; to cover such details would be, I think, too long a task.

Comedy, as we said, is an imitation of men worse than the average, not indeed as regards any and every sort of vice, but only as regards the Ridiculous, which is a species

[1] Costumes, masks, etc.

of the Ugly. The Ridiculous may be defined as a mistake or deformity which produces no pain or harm to others; the comic mask, for example, which induces laughter, is something ugly and distorted, but gives rise to no pain.

The successive changes in Tragedy and their respective authors are well known. But the same cannot be said of Comedy; its early stages passed unnoticed because it was not as yet taken up in a serious way. [1449^b] It was not until late that the archon granted a chorus of comedians, who used to be mere volunteers. Comedy had already certain definite forms at the time when the record of those termed comic poets begins; but we do not know who first introduced masks, or prologues, or a plurality of actors and so forth. Epicharmus and Phormis, however, invented the Fable, i.e. the Plot, which is therefore of Sicilian origin; Crates was the first Athenian poet to abandon the Comedy of invective and devise stories of a general and non-personal nature, in other words Fables or Plots.

Epic poetry then has been seen to coincide with Tragedy in so far as it is an imitation of serious subjects in a lofty kind of verse. It differs from it, however, (1) in that it is in one kind of verse and in narrative form; and (2) in its length, which is due to its action having no set time-limit, whereas Tragedy endeavours to keep as far as possible within a single circuit of the sun, or something approximate to that. This, I say, is another point of difference between them, though the practice in this respect was originally the same in tragedies and in epic poems. Epic and Tragedy differ also (3) in their constituents, some being common to both and others peculiar to Tragedy; hence a judge of good and bad in Tragedy is a judge of those qualities in epic poetry too. All the parts of Epic are included in Tragedy, but not all those of Tragedy in Epic.

III. Tragedy

A. *The Definition and Constituent Elements of Tragedy*

We shall have something to say about Epic poetry and Comedy later on.[1] Let us now consider Tragedy; but before doing so we must formulate the definition resulting from our foregoing remarks.

A tragedy is the imitation of an action (1) that is serious, has magnitude,[2] and is complete in itself; (2) in language with pleasurable accessories, each kind introduced separately in different parts of the work; (3) in a dramatic as distinct from a narrative form; (4) with incidents arousing pity and fear, whereby to provide an outlet for such emotions. By 'language with pleasurable accessories' I mean that with rhythm and harmony or song superadded; and by 'each kind ... separately' I mean that in some portions verse only is employed, and in others song.

1. A tragedy must include (*a*) the Spectacle, i.e. the stage-appearance of the actors, because they act the stories; (*b*) Melody; (*c*) Diction, these two being the means of their imitation. Here by 'Diction' I mean simply the metrical composition. The meaning of 'Melody' is so obvious as to require no explanation.

Again, the subject represented is also an action; and the action involves agents, who must necessarily have their distinctive qualities, both of (*d*) Character and (*e*) Thought, [1450ᵃ] since it is on account of these that we ascribe certain qualities to their action. Consequently there are in the natural order of things two causes (character and thought) of their actions and therefore of their ultimate

[1] For the discussion of epic poetry *see* pages 42 ff.
[2] i.e. is sufficiently long and serious to be more than trivial.

success or failure in life.   Now the action, that which is done, is represented on the stage by (*f*) the Fable or Plot. The Plot, in our present sense of the word, is nothing more or less than the combination of the incidents or things done in the story; Character is what makes us ascribe certain moral qualities to the agents; and Thought is shown in all they say when proving a particular point or, perhaps, expressing a general truth.

Every tragedy, therefore, must contain six (and *only* six) parts which determine its quality.   They are Spectacle, Melody, Diction, Character, Thought, and Plot; two of them arise from the means, one from the manner, and three from the objects imitated.   Practically all dramatists have employed these formative constituents, for all plays alike admit of Spectacle, Melody, Diction, Character, Thought, and Plot.

2. The most important of these six is the Plot. Tragedy is an imitation not of persons but of action and life, of happiness and misery.   Now happiness and misery take the form of action; the end at which the dramatist aims is a certain kind of activity, not a quality. We have certain qualities in accordance with character, but it is in our actions that we are happy or the reverse. Actors therefore do not perform with a view to portraying character; no, they include character for the sake of the action.   Consequently the end of a tragedy is its action, i.e. its fable or plot; and the end is in all things paramount.   Moreover, there can be no tragedy without action, but there may be one without Character.   The tragedies of most modern dramatists are devoid of character—a defect common among poets of all kinds, and with its counterpart in painting in Zeuxis compared with Polygnotus; [1] for whereas Polygnotus excels in the

[1] Dr Hamilton Fyfe compares Lawrence and Raeburn with Zeuxis and Polygnotus respectively.

representation of character, Zeuxis has no such gift. Furthermore one may string together speeches that are well constructed from the viewpoint of Diction and Thought, and yet fail to achieve the true tragic effect; but one will be far more successful with a tragedy which, no matter how inferior in these respects, has a plot, i.e. a combination of incidents. Again, the most powerfully attractive elements in Tragedy, the Peripeties and Discoveries,[1] are parts of the plot. Yet another proof of the plot's pre-eminence is the fact that beginners succeed earlier with Diction and Character than with the construction of a story; and the same is true of almost all the early dramatists. Plot therefore is the first essential— the very soul, as it were, of Tragedy; Character comes second.[2] [1450^{b}3] Tragedy is an imitation of action; if it imitates the personal agents, it does so mainly for the sake of the action. Third comes Thought, by which I mean the power of saying whatever can be said, or what befits the occasion. In the speeches of a tragedy this is the function of the arts of Politics and Rhetoric;[3] the old tragedians make their personages talk like statesmen, and the moderns like rhetoricians. Thought is quite distinct from Character. Character in a tragedy is that which reveals the *will* of the agents, i.e. the kind of things they choose or reject, where that is not obvious.[4] Thought, on the other hand, is shown in all that is said by way of proving or disproving some particular point, or of enunciating some universal proposition. Fourth

[1] *See* page 20.
[2] You find the same sort of thing in painting: [1450 ^{b}] if an artist lays on even the most beautiful colours without order, he will not give the same pleasure as will be derived from a simple black-and-white sketch for a portrait.—(A.)
[3] *See* page 34.
[4] Hence there is no room for Character in a speech dealing with some matter that is quite indifferent.—(A.)

among the literary elements is Diction; I mean, as already explained, the expression of thoughts in words, which is more or less the same thing with verse as with prose. As for the remaining parts, Melody is the greatest of the pleasurable accessories. Spectacle is certainly an attraction, but it is the least artistic of all the parts and has least connection with the art of poetry. The tragic effect is possible without a public performance and actors; besides, the organization of Spectacle is more a matter for the costumier than the poet.

B. *The Proper Length of a Tragic Play*

Having distinguished the several parts, let us now go on to explain how the Plot should be constructed, because that is the first and most important thing in Tragedy. We have decided that a tragedy is an imitation of an action that is a whole and complete in itself, and *of some magnitude*; for a whole may have no magnitude worth consideration. Now a whole is that which has beginning, middle, and end. A beginning is that which is not itself necessarily after anything else, and which has naturally something else after it; an end, on the contrary, is that which is naturally after something itself, either as its necessary or as its usual sequel, and with nothing else after it; and a middle is that which is by its very nature after one thing and has another after itself. A well constructed plot, therefore, must not begin or end at any random point; it must make use of beginning and end as just described. Again, in order to be beautiful, a living creature, and indeed every whole consisting of parts, must not only possess a certain order in the arrangement of its parts, but must also be of a certain definite magnitude. Beauty depends on two conditions—size and order; it is therefore impossible either (*a*) in a very minute creature, since our perception becomes indistinct as it approaches instantaneity; or (b) in a creature of enormous size (say 100 miles long), [1451ᵃ] because in that case the object is not seen all at once—its unity and wholeness are lost to the beholder. Just in the same way then as a beautiful whole made up of parts, or a beautiful living creature, must have some size, and a size easily taken in as a whole by the eye, so also a dramatic plot must have some length within the range of memory.[1] With the limit of its length, so far as concerns a stage-performance before an audience, the theory of poetry is not concerned. If the performers had to act a hundred tragedies, they would be timed by water-clocks, as is done on certain other occasions.[2] The limit, however, fixed by the nature of the thing is this: the longer the story, consistently with its being comprehensible as a whole, the finer it is by reason of its magnitude. Roughly speaking, one may define the magnitude of a plot as sufficient if the period allows the hero to pass by a series of probable or necessary stages from happiness to misfortune, or *vice versa*.

C. *Unity of Plot*

1. This does not consist, as some suppose, in its having one man as its subject. A whole host of things happen to one man, some of which cannot be worked into a unity; and likewise one man does many things which cannot be reduced to a single action. Hence the obvious mistake of all those poets who have written a *Heracleid*, a *Theseid*, or similar poems; they think that because Heracles was one man his story too must be one story. Homer, on the other hand, was evidently quite clear on this point,

[1] It must not be so long that the beginning is forgotten before the end is reached—like some Chinese plays.

[2] In the law-courts speeches were limited by water-clocks. See *Ath. Con.* 67.

whether by art or instinct, just as he excels in every other respect. In writing the *Odyssey* he did not include all the hero's adventures; e.g. his being wounded on Parnassus and his pretending to be mad when called up for military service, neither of which incidents had any probable or necessary connection with the other. No, what Homer did in the *Odyssey*, as also in the *Iliad*, was to take an action with a unity such as we are describing. The fact is that, just as in the other imitative arts one imitation is invariably of a single thing, so in poetry the story, as an imitation of action, must represent one action, a complete whole; and it must connect the various incidents in such a way that the whole will be disjoined and dislocated if any one of them is transposed or removed. For that which makes an apparent difference by its presence or absence is no genuine part of the whole.

2. It is clear from what has been said [1] that the poet's function is to describe not what *has* happened, but the kind of thing that *might* happen, i.e. what is possible as being probable or necessary. [1451ᵇ] The historian and the poet differ from one another not by virtue of the fact that one is writing prose and the other verse; it would be possible to produce a metrical version of Herodotus, but the result would still be a species of history. Where the historian really differs from the poet is in his describing what has happened, while the other describes the kind of thing that might happen. Poetry therefore is more philosophic and of greater significance than history, for its statements are of the nature rather of universals, whereas those of history are particulars. A universal statement declares what such or such a kind of man will probably or necessarily say or do; and that is the aim of poetry, though it affixes proper names to the characters.

[1] In the remainder of this section (C) Aristotle shows that unity of form is attained by making the story's content 'universal'.

A particular statement says what, for example, Alcibiades did or suffered. In Comedy this is clear now that the New has superseded the Old; it is only when their plot is already made up of probable incidents that the comic writers give a basis of proper names, choosing for the purpose any names that may occur to them, instead of writing like the old iambic poets about particular individuals. Tragic poets, however, continue to hold fast by the historic names. The reason is that what convinces is the possible; now while we are not yet sure as to the possibility of that which has not happened, that which *has* happened is manifestly possible, otherwise it would not have come to pass. Nevertheless even in Tragedy there are some plays which have only one or two known names, the remainder being inventions. There are others which have no known names at all, e.g. Agathon's *Antheus*; here both names and incidents are of the poet's invention, but the play is no less delightful on that account. There is consequently no need to aim at a strict adherence to the traditional stories with which tragedies deal. It would be absurd in fact to do so, since even the known stories are known to only a few, though they are a delight none the less to all.

It is clear from the foregoing that the poet must be the poet or maker of his plots rather than of his verses, because he is a poet by virtue of the imitative element in his work, and it is actions that he imitates. Even if he happens to take a subject from actual fact he is none the less a poet; for there is nothing to prevent some historical occurrences from being in the probable and possible order of things, and it is in virtue of *that* that he is their poet or maker. [1]

---

[1] Certain historical occurrences seem improbable, and even impossible, until a poet (like a modern historian) 'makes' the story by showing the course of events.

Of simple plots and actions the episodic are the worst. By an episodic plot I mean one in which the episodes do not follow one upon another in accordance with probability or necessity. Actions of this kind are constructed by bad poets through their own fault, and by good ones on account of the players. Because his work is destined for performance in the theatre, a good poet often stretches out a plot beyond what it will bear, [1452ᵃ] and is thus compelled to twist the sequence of incidents.

Tragedy, however, is an imitation not only of a complete action, but also of incidents that arouse pity and fear. These incidents make the strongest impact when they occur unexpectedly and at the same time in consequence of one another; in such circumstances they contain a greater element of the marvellous than if they happened by themselves or by mere chance. Even chance events seem most marvellous if they appear to have a background of design, as for example the statue of Mitys at Argos killing the man responsible for Mitys' death, by falling on him as he watched a public spectacle; [1] for we consider such incidents to be not devoid of meaning. A plot of this kind, therefore, is necessarily finer than others.

D. Simple and Complex Plots. Peripety. Discovery

1. Some plots are simple and others complex, because the actions they represent are naturally one or the other. By a simple action I mean one that proceeds in the way defined as a continuous whole, when the change in the hero's fortunes takes place without Peripety or Discovery; by a complex action, one that involves Peripety, Discovery, or both. Both these should arise from the structure of the plot itself, so as to be the necessary or

---

[1] See Plutarch, De sera num. vind. 553 D.

probable consequence of what has gone before. There is a world of difference between a thing happening *propter hoc* and *post hoc*.

2. Peripety is the change as described above [1] from one state of things in a play to its opposite, and that too in the way we are saying, in the probable or necessary sequence of events. It is thus, for example, in the *Oedipus*; here the opposite state of things is effected by the messenger, who, coming to congratulate Oedipus and remove his fears on the subject of his mother, reveals the secret of his birth. So too in *Lynceus*: [2] just as Abas is being led to execution, accompanied by Danaus who will put him to death, the incidents preceding this result in his being saved and Danaus perishing instead.

3. Discovery, as the very word implies, is a change from ignorance to knowledge, and consequently either to love or to hate, in the personages destined for good or evil fortune. The finest form of Discovery is one accompanied by peripeties, such as occurs in *Oedipus*. There are, of course, other forms of Discovery: what we have said happens sometimes and in a sense with reference to inanimate things, even things of a casual sort; and it is also possible to discover whether someone has or has not done something. But the form most closely connected with the plot and the action of the play is the one first mentioned. This kind of discovery, with a peripety, [1452ᵇ] will give rise either to pity or to fear—actions of that nature being what Tragedy is assumed to represent; and it will also contribute to bringing about a happy or unhappy ending. Well then, the discovery is of persons. It may be that of one party only to the other, the latter being already known; or both parties may have to make

---

[1] Page 16: 'from happiness to misfortune or *vice versa*'.
[2] By Theodectes, fourth century B.C.

themselves known, as Iphigeneia was revealed to Orestes by sending the letter while another discovery was necessary in order to reveal him to Iphigeneia.[1]

Two parts of the plot then, Peripety and Discovery, are concerned with matters of this kind. A third part is Suffering, which may be defined as a destructive or painful action, e.g. murders on the stage, tortures, woundings, and the like. The other two have already been explained.[2]

E. *The Aim of Tragedy and the Conditions on which its Effect depends*

After what has been said above, our next points for discussion will be: (*a*) At what should the poet aim, and what should he avoid, in constructing his plots? and (*b*) What are the conditions upon which the effect of Tragedy depends?

(*a*) The plot, in the finest form of Tragedy, must not be simple but complex; and further, it must imitate actions that arouse pity and fear. Consequently (i) a good man must not be shown as passing from happiness to misfortune; for that does not inspire pity or fear, but is an outrage upon our moral feeling. Nor (ii) must a bad man be seen passing from misfortune to happiness. That is as untragic as can possibly be; it makes no appeal either to our sense of poetic justice, [1453ª] or to our pity, or to our fear. Nor (iii) should an extremely bad man be depicted as falling from happiness into misfortune. Such a story may stir the human feeling in us, but not our pity or fear; pity is reserved for undeserved

---

[1] The reference is to Euripides' *Iphigeneia in Tauris*, 727 ff.

[2] The next section, [1452ᵇ14–27], is probably an interpolated fragment, though undoubtedly by Aristotle. I have placed it as an appendix (page 57).

misfortune, and fear for the misfortune of a man like ourselves; so there will be nothing conducive to pity or fear in a situation of that kind. There remains then the intermediate sort of person, one who is not pre-eminently virtuous and just, one who incurs misfortune not as a result of vice or depravity, but by some error of judgment while enjoying great reputation and prosperity. You have examples in Oedipus, Thyestes, and distinguished men of similar families. The sound plot, therefore, must have a single, and not (as some maintain) a double issue; the hero's change of fortune must be not from misery to happiness, but the other way round; and it must be due not to any depravity, but to some grave mistake on the part of a man such as we have described, or better—certainly not worse—than that. Facts, too, bear witness to our theory. Though the poets began by accepting any tragic story available, in these days the finest tragedies are invariably written on the story of a few families, on that of Alcmaeon, Oedipus, Orestes, Meleager, Thyestes, Telephus, or any others that may have been involved, whether as agents or sufferers, in some hideous deed. The tragedy then that is theoretically the best has a plot of this kind. The critics,[1] therefore, are wrong who blame Euripides for following this course in his tragedies, many of which have an unhappy ending. It is, as we have said, the right and proper course; and here now is the strongest proof. On the stage at public performances such plays, when correctly worked out, are seen to be the most truly tragic; and Euripides, even though his execution leaves much to be desired in other respects,[2] must be recognized as undoubtedly the most tragic of dramatists. Next comes the sort of plot which some put first: one with a double

[1] Of whom Aristophanes is the most famous.
[2] See pages 26, 33.

story, like the *Odyssey*, and an opposite issue for the good and bad personages.[1] It is ranked as first only because audiences are so weak;[2] the poets simply follow their public, writing to suit its whims. But the pleasure here is not that of Tragedy; it belongs rather to Comedy. The most determined enemies in the play, e.g. Orestes and Aegisthus, march off good friends at the conclusion, and no one is slain by anyone.

[1453b] Fear and pity may be aroused by Spectacle,[3] but they may also be aroused by the very structure of the incidents—which is the better way and indicative of the better poet. The plot, in fact, should be constructed in such a way that, even without seeing the things take place, he who simply *hears the account* of them shall be filled with horror and pity at the incidents; and those feelings are just what one would experience at the mere recital of the story of Oedipus. To produce this effect by means of Spectacle is less artistic and requires extraneous assistance.[4] Those who employ Spectacle to parade what is merely monstrous and not productive of fear have no share in the art of tragedy; one must not expect every kind of pleasure from a tragedy, but only its own distinctive pleasure.

(*b*) Since the poet has to employ imitation in order to produce the pleasure arising from pity and fear, it is evident that the causes of pity and fear must be worked into the incidents of his story. Let us see then what kinds of incident strike one as horrible, or rather as piteous. In deeds of this sort the parties must necessarily be either friends, or enemies, or indifferent to one another. Now when such a deed is perpetrated by enemy

[1] *See* page 21.
[2] i.e. they cannot appreciate the strong situations of great tragedy.
[3] i.e. the mere sight of disaster.
[4] In the form of scenery, make-up, etc.

upon enemy, there is nothing to arouse our pity either in his doing or in his purposing to do it, except in so far as the actual pain of the sufferer is concerned; and the same is true when the parties are neither friends nor enemies. But whenever the deed is done within a family—when murder or the like is committed or meditated by brother on brother,[1] by son on father,[2] by mother on son,[3] or by son on mother[4]—these are the situations of which the poet should take advantage. There must accordingly be no interference with the traditional stories, e.g. the murder of Clytaemnestra by Orestes and of Eriphyle by Alcmaeon. Even so the poet still has some field for originality; it is for him to devise the right way of handling these stories. Let us explain more clearly what we mean by the 'right way'. The dreadful deed may be done with malice aforethought, as in the old poets, and in Medea's murder of her children in Euripides. Or the perpetrator may act unaware of his relationship, which he does not discover until later, as does Oedipus in Sophocles. In this last case the deed is outside the play; but it may take place within it, like Alcmaeon in Astydamas' tragedy, or that of Telegonus in *Odysseus Wounded*.[5] Thirdly it is possible for one meditating some deadly injury to another, in ignorance of his relationship, to make the discovery before actually committing the crime. No other situations are possible, since the deed must of necessity be either done or not done, and either wittingly or unwittingly.

The worst situation is when someone is with full knowledge on the point of doing the deed, and then leaves it

---

[1] e.g. Eteocles and Polyneices in the *Phoenissae* of Euripides.

[2] e.g. Oedipus and Laius in Sophocles' *Oedipus Tyrannus*.

[3] e.g. Althaea and Meleager.

[4] e.g. Orestes and Clytaemnestra in the *Choephoroi* of Aeschylus and in the *Electra* of Sophocles and of Euripides.

[5] Probably Sophocles' lost *Odysseus Thorn-struck*.

undone. That situation offends our moral sensibilities and is at the same time, through the absence of suffering, untragic. Hence no one [1454ᵃ] is represented as acting thus, except in a few instances, e.g. Haemon and Creon in *Antigone*.[1] Next comes the actual perpetration of a premeditated deed. A better situation than that, however, is for the deed to be done in ignorance and the relationship discovered afterwards; for there is nothing offensive about it, and the discovery will serve to astound us. But the best of all is the last, as exemplified for instance in the *Cresphontes*,[2] where Merope is about to slay her son, but recognizes him just in time to stay her hand; in *Iphigeneia*,[3] where sister and brother are similarly placed; or in *Helle*,[4] where the son recognizes his mother when on the point of surrendering her to her enemy.

This is the reason why our tragedies are confined, as we said above, to so few families. It was accident rather than art that led poets in quest of subjects to embody this kind of incident in their plots. They are still obliged, therefore, to make use of families in which such things have occurred. Enough has now been said [5] about constructing the plot and the kind of plot needed for Tragedy.

F. Delineation of Character

As regards Character, there are four points at which the poet must aim. (1) All the characters should be good. The play will have an element of Character if, as has been said,[6] what a personage says or does reveals a certain

[1] Sophocles, *Antigone*, 1231.
[2] A lost play by Euripides.
[3] Euripides' *Iphigeneia in Tauris*.
[4] An unknown play.
[5] But *see* section *G* below, page 28.
[6] *See* page 12.

moral purpose; and it will have a *good* element of Character if the purpose thus revealed is good.   Such goodness is possible in every type of person, even in a woman or a slave, though the one is of course an inferior and the other a worthless being.   (2) All the characters should be appropriate.   There is, for example, such a thing as a manly character; but neither manliness nor cleverness is appropriate in a female character.   (3) All the characters should be like the original.   This is not the same as their being good and appropriate, in the present sense of the latter term.   (4) All the characters should remain consistent throughout the play; if the original to be imitated is inconsistent, then his character should be consistently inconsistent.   We have an example of baseness of character, not required for the story, in Menelaus in the *Orestes*; [1] of the incongruous and inappropriate in the lamentation of Odysseus in *Scylla*,[2] as also in the rationalistic argument of Melanippe; [3] and of inconsistency in *Iphigeneia at Aulis*, where Iphigeneia the suppliant bears no resemblance to the later Iphigeneia.

In character-drawing, as in putting together the incidents of a play, what one should do is to keep an eye always on the necessary or the probable; so that whenever such-and-such a personage says or does such-and-such a thing it shall be the probable or necessary result of his character, and whenever such-and-such an incident follows upon such-and-such another it shall do so as the necessary or probable consequence thereof.

Hence it is clear [4] that the denouement also should

---

[1] By Euripides.

[2] A dithyramb by Timotheus (446–357 B.C.).

[3] In Euripides' lost *Melanippe the Learned*, where she argued against the popular idea of monsters in a manner unbecoming a woman, according to Aristotle's view.

[4] This paragraph is a digression; in the next Aristotle returns to the subject of Character.

[1454ᵇ] arise from the plot itself and not depend upon a mechanical contrivance,[1] as in *Medea* or in the story of the arrested departure of the Greeks in the *Iliad*.[2] Such a contrivance may be used only for matters outside the play—for past events beyond human knowledge, or for future events which need to be foretold or announced; for we recognize that the gods know everything. None of the incidents should be improbable; but if this rule cannot be observed, any improbability should lie outside the tragedy, like the one in Sophocles' *Oedipus*.[3]

As Tragedy is an imitation of persons better than the average man, we poets should follow the example of good portrait-painters, who reproduce a man's distinctive features, and at the same time make him better looking than he really is without departing from his true likeness. So too the poet, when portraying men too quick or too slow to anger, or with similar defects of character, must know how to represent them as such, yet at the same time as good men, as Agathon and Homer have represented Achilles.

The foregoing rules must be constantly borne in mind; and so must those for such points of stage-effect as directly depend on the art of the dramatist,[4] since in these too it is often possible to miss the mark. However, I have dealt at length with this matter in one of my published works.[5]

---

[1] e.g. the *deus ex machina.*

[2] *Il.* ii. 155.

[3] It seems unlikely that Oedipus, seeking to discover who had slain Laius, should have overlooked the clue provided by the murder which he himself had committed.

[4] As distinct from the actors, costumiers, scene-painters, etc.

[5] The lost dialogue *On Poets.*

G. Supplementary Remarks on Plot [1]

1. Discovery in general we have already explained.[2] First among its species is (a) the least artistic but one which the poets most frequently use through lack of originality. I refer to discovery by signs or marks. Some of these are congenital, e.g. 'the lance-head with which the Earth-born are marked',[3] or stars,[4] such as Carcinus introduces in his *Thyestes*. Others are acquired after birth, and these are either (i) marks on the body, e.g. scars, or (ii) external tokens such as necklaces, or, to take another sort of example, the ark whereby the twins were discovered in *Tyro*.[5] Even these, however, may be used with varying effect. The discovery of Odysseus through his scar was made in one way by the nurse and in another by the swineherd.[6] Now a discovery in which marks or signs are used to prove one's own identity is less artistic, as indeed are all such; one that arises suddenly and unexpectedly, as in the Bath-story, are of a better order. Next come (b) discoveries which are made directly by the poet and are therefore inartistic. Thus in *Iphigeneia in Tauris* Orestes discovers himself; whereas his sister reveals her identity through the letter, Orestes himself says what is demanded by the poet but not by the story. This therefore is somewhat akin to the

[1] These discuss a series of points and rules of construction which were omitted in Aristotle's sketch of the general theory of Plot.

[2] Page 20.

[3] From an unknown play. The reference is to the mark said to have been visible on the Spartoi or Earth-born at Thebes.

[4] This mark was inherited by the descendants of Pelops as a legacy of his ivory shoulder.

[5] A lost play by Sophocles. Tyro's twins by Poseidon were discovered in an ark or floating cradle on the Enipeus.

[6] *Od.* xix. 392. The nurse Eurycleia made the discovery for herself while bathing him; Odysseus himself pointed out the scar to the swineherd—a means of discovery which, Aristotle goes on to explain, is less satisfactory.

defect already mentioned, since he might have put forward certain tokens as well. Another example is the
'voice of the shuttle' in Sophocles' *Tereus*.[1] A third
species (*c*) is discovery through memory, from a man's
consciousness being reawakened [1455ª] by something
seen or heard. In the *Cyprioi* of Dicaeogenes, for
instance, the sight of a picture causes a man to burst
into tears;[2] and in the 'Tale of Alcinous',[3] Odysseus,
hearing the harper, recalls the past and weeps. Tears
were in each case the means of discovery. A fourth
kind (*d*) is discovery through deductive reasoning. Thus
in the *Choephoroi*[4] we have: 'Someone like me is here;
none but Orestes is like me; therefore he must be here'.
Another example would be the line of argument suggested
by Polyidus the Sophist for the *Iphigeneia*; he observed
that it would have been only natural for Orestes to
reflect: 'My sister was sacrificed, and now I too am going
to be sacrificed'.[5] Or that in the *Tydeus* of Theodectes:
'I came to find a son, and am to lose my own life'. Or
that in the *Phineidai*:[6] on seeing the place the women
realized what was to be their doom, since it was there
they had been exposed to die as unwanted children.
There is also (*e*) a composite discovery arising from an
erroneous inference by one party.[7] An example occurs
in *Odysseus the False Messenger*:[8] he said he would know

[1] The 'voice of the shuttle' refers to the embroidered picture
whereby Philomela, after being deprived of her tongue, told her
sister Procne the story of her rape by Tereus.

[2] Teucer came to Salamis in disguise and saw a picture of his
father, Telamon; he burst into tears and was thereby recognized.

[3] *Od.* viii. 521 ff.

[4] Aeschylus, *Choephoroi*, 168–234.

[5] And thus reveal himself by drawing her attention to the
strange coincidence.

[6] Nothing more is known about the *Tydeus* or the *Phineidai*.

[7] Possibly what is called to-day 'discovery by bluff'; but the
meaning of the passage is obscure.

[8] Nothing more is known about this play.

a bow, which he had not seen, but to conclude from that that he would know it again (as though he had once seen it) was an erroneous inference. The best of all discoveries, however, is (*f*) that which arises from the incidents themselves, when the great surprise occurs as the result of a probable incident, like that in the *Oedipus* of Sophocles—and also in *Iphigeneia*, where it was not at all unlikely that the heroine would wish to send a letter home. Discoveries of this last kind are the only ones that do not depend upon the artifice of signs, necklaces, etc. Next best are discoveries by reasoning.

2. When constructing his plots and forging the diction the poet must do his best (*a*) to visualize the actual scenes. In this way, seeing everything most vividly, as if he were an actual spectator of the events, he will be able to devise what is appropriate and be least likely to overlook incongruities. This appears from the fate of Carcinus, who was censured for the return of Amphiaraus from the sanctuary.[1] This would have escaped detection if it had not been actually witnessed by an audience; but on the stage his play was an utter failure, because the incongruity annoyed the spectators.

If possible, the poet should even (*b*) act his story with the very attitudes and gestures that his personages might be expected to use. Granted the same natural endowments, the dramatist who experiences the emotions described will be the most convincing; distress and anger, for instance, are portrayed most truthfully by one who feels them at the time of writing. This is why poetry requires a man with special gifts of nature and temperament, or else a touch of madness; [2] the former is highly impressionable, while the latter is beside himself with emotion.

---

[1] In a lost play. Cf. Aristotle's criticism of the pursuit of Hector (page 45).
[2] i.e. the 'frenzy' of inspiration.

(c) Again, as regards his story, [1455ᵇ] whether it be
ready made or of his own invention, the poet should first
reduce it to its simplest terms before proceeding to insert
episodes.   By way of illustrating what I mean, take
Iphigeneia in Tauris.   Here it is, reduced to its simplest
terms: A certain maiden having been offered in sacrifice,
but invisibly snatched from her sacrificers and trans-
ported to another country where custom dictated that all
strangers should be sacrificed to the Goddess, was
appointed priestess of this rite.   Long afterwards her
brother unexpectedly turned up, the why and wherefore
of his journey on the orders of an oracle being outside the
plot.   On arrival he was arrested, and about to be sacrificed, when he disclosed his identity—either as Euripides
describes it, or (as Polyidus suggested) by the not improbable remark that he too was doomed to be sacrificed
as his sister had been—and the disclosure led to his
salvation.   Now then, having got that far, the next
thing, after assigning proper names, is to work in accessory incidents.   One must, however, take care that those
incidents are appropriate, e.g. Orestes' fit of madness
which caused him to be arrested, and the purification
which effected his deliverance.   In plays then the episodes are brief, but in epic they are used to lengthen the
poem.   The *Odyssey* can be summarized quite briefly as
follows.   A certain man has been abroad for many years;
Poseidon is lying in wait for him, and he is all alone.
Matters at home, too, have reached the point at which his
property is being squandered and his son's death plotted
by suitors to his wife.   He himself arrives there after
terrible sufferings, reveals himself, and falls upon his
enemies.   The story concludes with his salvation and
their destruction.   This is all that is proper to the
Odyssey; the rest is episode.

(d) Every tragedy is in part Complication and in part

Denouement. The complication consists of incidents that have taken place before the opening of the play and often some also of those that occur within it; the remainder form the denouement. By complication I mean everything from the beginning of the story up to the point where the hero suffers a change of fortune; by denouement, everything from the latter point to the end. In the *Lynceus* of Theodectes, for example, the complication includes both the incidents which are supposed to have happened before the beginning of the play, and also the seizure of the child [1] and then that of his parents; the denouement everything from the indictment for murder to the end. Now it is right to describe a tragedy as the same as or different from another chiefly on the basis of their plots, i.e. that they have or have not the same complication and denouement. There are many dramatists who produce a good complication, but a bad denouement. It is important, however, that both should be properly mastered.

(*e*) There are four species of Tragedy, each arising through the prominence in it of one of the constituent elements we have mentioned: (i) The complex tragedy, which is all peripety and discovery; (ii) the tragedy of suffering, e.g. [1456ᵃ] the *Ajaxes* and *Ixions*; (iii) the tragedy of character, e.g. the *Women of Phthia* and *Peleus*; [2] (iv) that in which spectacle is predominant, examples of which are the *Daughters of Phorcys*, *Prometheus*,[3] and all plays whose scene is the underworld. The poet should accordingly strive to combine all four elements of interest, or at any rate the most important and greatest possible number of them. This is particularly

[1] Abas, son of Lynceus and Danaus' daughter Hypermestra. The play is lost.

[2] The first of these was by Sophocles; both he and Euripides wrote a *Peleus*. All are lost.

[3] Both lost satyr plays by Aeschylus.

necessary nowadays, when poets are the victims of unfair criticism. Just because there have been earlier dramatists who excelled in the several species of Tragedy, every one of their modern counterparts is expected to outdo each of his predecessors in the latter's strongest point.

(*f*) A poet should remember what we have already said, and not write a tragedy on an epic body of incident (i.e. one containing a plurality of stories), by attempting to dramatize, for instance, the entire story of the *Iliad*. In that work, because of its scale, every part is treated at proper length; but the result of a drama on the same story is most disappointing. There is evidence of this in the fact that all who have dramatized the entire story of Ilium's fall, and not part by part, like Euripides—or the whole of the Niobe legend, instead of a portion, like Aeschylus—either come to grief altogether or at any rate meet with a cool reception on the stage. It was when he neglected this rule, and this alone, that even Agathon failed. Yet in their peripeties, as also in their simple plots, the poets I mean work wonders in aiming at the effects they desire—a tragic situation and one that makes an appeal to our human feelings, like the clever rogue (e.g. Sisyphus) deceived, or the brave sinner worsted. This is probable, however, only in Agathon's sense, when he refers to the probability of even improbabilities coming to pass.

(*g*) The Chorus should be regarded as one of the actors; it should form part and parcel of the whole, and take a share in the action. This it does in the tragedies of Sophocles rather than in those of Euripides. But if we consider a play by any of the later dramatists, we shall find that its choral parts have no more to do with the plot than with that of any other tragedy. Hence the modern practice of singing mere interludes, which was started by Agathon. And yet what difference is there

between singing such choral interludes and grafting a
speech (or even an entire act) from one play on to
another?

H. *Thought and Diction*

1. Having discussed Plot and Character, it remains
for us to say something about Thought and Diction in
Tragedy.   As regards Thought, I refer you to what I
said in the lectures on Rhetoric, to which field of inquiry
it more properly belongs.   The thought of the persons in
a play is revealed in all that must be effected by their
language: in every attempt to prove or disprove, to
arouse emotion (pity, fear, anger, and the like), [1456^b]
or to exaggerate or belittle things.   It is clear also that
the same rules apply to actions or incidents as to ideas
and their expression, whenever it is intended to arouse
pity or horror, or to produce an effect of importance or
probability.   The only difference is that in action the
effect has to be produced by the situation alone, whereas
in the case of the spoken word it has to be produced by
the speaker and result from his language.   What indeed
would be the use of the speaker if things appeared as if
intended quite apart from what he says?

As regards Diction, one line of inquiry is the way in
which the meaning is affected by the use of different
moods, tenses, etc.; e.g. the difference between command
and prayer, simple statement and threat, question and
answer, and so forth.   Such matters, however, come
within the province of Elocution and the professors of
that art.   Whether the poet knows these things or not,
his art as a poet is never seriously criticized on that
account.   What fault is there to find with Homer's 'Sing
of the wrath, Goddess'? [1]—which Protagoras criticized

[1] The first words of the *Iliad*.

as being a command where the author intended a
prayer, since to bid someone do or not do, he says, is a
command. Let us pass over this, then, as belonging to
an art other than poetry.[1]

2. [1458a31] There are two kinds of nouns: [2] (a) simple,
i.e. made up of non-significant parts, like the word
'earth', or (b) double; in the latter case the word may
consist either (i) of a significant and a non-significant
part (a distinction which disappears in the compound),
or (ii) of two significant parts.[3] It is possible also to have
triple, quadruple, and even larger compounds, like most
amplified proper names, e.g. *Hermocaicoxanthus*.[4]

Every noun, regardless of its structure, is either (a) the
ordinary word for a thing, (b) a strange word, (c) a metaphor, (d) an ornamental word, (e) a coined word, (f) a
word expanded, or (g) curtailed or (h) altered in form.[5]

By the ordinary word I mean that in general use in a
country; by a strange word, one used elsewhere. It is
clear then that the same word can be both strange and
ordinary, though not with reference to the same people;
sigunos,[6] for instance, is an ordinary word among the
Cypriots, but strange in Athenian ears.

---

[1] The next section of the original, [1456b20–57a30], is recognized
by most scholars as an interpolation. I have accordingly placed
it as an appendix (page 58).

[2] 'Nouns' here and in Appendix II includes not only what we
mean by the word, but also adjectives, personal and demon-
strative pronouns, verbs when they stand alone as mere names
for actions, and possibly even the definite article.

[3] Dr Hamilton Fyfe gives as an example of (i) 'cur-tain'; *tain*
is non-significant, *cur* has a meaning, but not in this compound.
His example of (ii) is 'tooth-brush', where both parts are significant.

[4] A compound of three river names: Hermus, Caicus, and
Xanthus, used perhaps as the epithet of a god.

[5] Aristotle now proceeds to deal with all these. His explanation
of the 'ornamental word', however, has been lost.

[6] Meaning a spear.

Metaphor consists in giving a thing the name that belongs properly to something else, the transference being either (i) from genus to species, or (ii) from species to genus, (iii) from species to species, or (iv) on grounds of analogy. (i) That from genus to species may be illustrated by 'Here stands my ship', for lying at anchor is a particular kind of 'standing'. (ii) That from species to genus by 'Truly ten thousand good deeds Odysseus hath wrought', where 'ten thousand', which is a particular large number is used instead of the generic 'a large number'. That from species to species by 'Drawing the life with the bronze', and by 'Severing with the enduring bronze'; [1] here 'draw' is used in the sense of 'sever' and 'sever' in that of 'draw', both words meaning to 'take away' something. The transference on grounds of analogy is possible when four terms are related in such a way that the second is to the first as the fourth to the third, and *vice versa*. Occasionally also one qualifies the metaphor by adding on to it that to which the word it supplants is relative. Thus a cup is relative to Dionysus as a shield is to Ares. The cup will accordingly be described as the 'shield *of Dionysus*', and the shield as the 'cup *of Ares*'. To take another example: Old age is to life, as evening is to day; so evening will be described as the 'old age *of the day*' (or by the Empedoclean equivalent [2]), and old age as the 'evening' or 'sunset *of life*'. Some terms related in this way have no special name of their own, but they will none the less be metaphorically described in the same way. Thus to cast forth seed-corn is called 'sowing'; but to cast forth flame, as in the case of the sun, has no special name. This nameless act, however, stands in exactly the same relation to sunlight

---

[1] In 'drawing' and 'severing' Aristotle is probably thinking of the cupping-bowl and the surgeon's knife.

[2] Unknown.

as sowing does to seed-corn. Hence the poet's phrase,
'sowing a god-created *flame*'.[1] There is yet another way
of handling metaphor along these lines. Having given
the thing the alien name, one may deny it one of the
attributes naturally associated with that name; one may,
for instance, call the shield not the 'cup *of Ares*', but a
'*w neless* cup'.

A coined word is one which, being quite unknown
among a people, is given to them by the poet himself;
e.g. (for there are certain words that appear to have
originated in this way) *ernuges* [2] for horns, and *arētēr* [3]
for priest.

[1458ª] A word is said to be lengthened out when it has
a short vowel made long or an extra syllable inserted; e.g.
poleōs for *poleós*, *Pēlēiadeō* for *Pēleidou*. It is said to be
curtailed when it has lost a part; e.g. *kri*, *dō*, and *ops* in
mia ginetai amphoterōn ops. It is an altered word when
part is left in its original form and part is fashioned by
the poet; e.g. *dexiteron* for *dexion*, in *dexiteron kata mazon*.

Nouns themselves are either masculine, feminine, or
neuter. All those which end in N, R, or S, or in the two
compounds of this last, PS and KS, are masculine.[4] All
those which end in the invariably long vowels Ē and Ō
and in A among the vowels capable of being lengthened,
are feminine. Consequently there is an equal number of
masculine and feminine endings, PS and KS being the
same as S. No noun ends in a mute or in either of the
two short vowels Ĕ and Ŏ. Only three (*meli*, *kommi*,

---

[1] Probably from a lost tragedy.

[2] i.e. 'sprouters'.

[3] A pray-er.

[4] There are, of course, neuters which end in PS and KS. But
Aristotle conceived neuters not as having terminations peculiar
to themselves, but as intermediate between masculine and
feminine, some of them having a masculine and others a feminine
ending.

peperi) end in I, and five in U.[1]   The intermediates, or neuters, end in the variable vowels or in N, R, or S.

3. Diction is perfect when it is clear and at the same time not mean.   The very clearest is that made up of the ordinary words for things, but its meanness is exhibited in the poetry of Cleophon and Sthenelus.[2]   On the other hand Diction becomes lofty and far removed from the prosaic when it makes use of unfamiliar terms, by which I mean strange words, metaphors, lengthened forms, and everything remote from the ordinary.   But a whole passage written in such terms will be either a riddle or gibberish; a riddle if made up of metaphors, gibberish if made up of strange words.   The very nature indeed of a riddle is this, to describe a fact in an impossible combination of words;[3] e.g. 'I saw a man glue brass on another with fire',[4] and so forth.   Gibberish results from the corresponding use of strange words.

Well then, a certain admixture of unfamiliar terms is required.   Such things as the strange word, the metaphor, the ornamental word, etc., will prevent the language from becoming prosaic and mean, while its quota of ordinary words will ensure clarity.   But what helps most to [1458ᵇ] render the diction at once clear and non-prosaic is the introduction of lengthened, curtailed, and altered forms of words.   Differing from the ordinary run of words, they will make the language unlike that in

[1] Bywater pointed out that the nouns ending in U are certainly more than five.   He suggests that Aristotle may have reached this number by omitting antiquated words and taking into account only those of current Attic usage.

[2] Aristophanes in the *Wasps* declares the diction of Sthenelus to be unpalatable without salt and vinegar.   Cleophon's was evidently on a level with his characters (*see* page 5).

[3] This cannot be done with the real names of things, but it can with their metaphorical substitutes.—(A.)

[4] The reference is to the use of a brass cupping bowl, which was applied to the punctured limb and heated, so as to create a vacuum.

everyday use, and thereby give it a non-prosaic appearance; but at the same time their possession of something in common with general usage will endow it with clarity. It is wrong therefore to condemn these modes of speech and ridicule the poet who employs them.   This was done, for example, by the elder Euclid; [1] he said it was easy to write poetry if one were to be allowed to lengthen out the words to any extent one pleased in this style, and he parodied the following sentences accordingly: *Epikharēn eidon Marathōnade badizonta*, and *ouk an g'eramenos ton ekeinou elleborou*.[2]   Too blatant a use of such licences has undoubtedly a ludicrous effect.   But the rule of moderation does not apply to them alone; it holds good in every department of poetic language.   If a tragic author uses metaphors, strange words, and the rest improperly and with a view to provoking mirth, the effect will be the same.   A proper use of them is a very different thing, as may be seen by taking an epic verse and seeing how it reads after the introduction of the normal words. The same should be done too with strange words, metaphor and the rest; one need only substitute the ordinary words to see the truth of what we are saying. There is, for example, an iambic which occurs in both Aeschylus and Euripides, and as it stands in the former it is a quite undistinguished line; whereas Euripides, by changing a single word, i.e. by substituting a strange term for what is recognized as the ordinary word, makes it appear a fine one.   Aeschylus in his *Philoctetes* [3] wrote:

phagedaina hē mou sarkas esthiei podos,

[1] Nothing certain is known about him.   Bywater suggested that he may be the Euclid who was archon eponymous in 503 B.C., in which year the reformed alphabet was officially adopted in Athens.

[2] These two bits of prose (their meaning is irrelevant) could be made, by a liberal use of 'lengthening out', etc., to read as hexameter verses.

[3] A lost play.

and here Euripides has merely altered *esthiei* into *thoinatai*.[1] Or suppose the line

    nun de m'eōn oligos te kai outidanos kai aeikēs [2]

to be altered by the substitution of ordinary words into

    nun de m'eōn mikros te kai asthenikos kai aeidēs.[3]

Or the line

    diphron aeikelion katatheis oligēn te trapezan [4]

into

    diphron mokhthēron katatheis mikran te trapezan.[5]

Or *ēiones boöōsin* [6] into *ēiones krazousin*.[7] Again, Ariphrades [8] used to ridicule the tragedians for using expressions unknown in the spoken language: *dōmatōn apo* (for *apo dōmatōn*), *sethen, egō de nin,* [1459a] *Akhilleōs peri* (for *peri Akhilleōs*), and so on. The very fact that all such terms and phrases are no part of common speech renders the diction non-prosaic; but Ariphrades was unaware of that. It is a great thing indeed to use these poetical forms, as well as compounds and strange words, in the proper way. But by far the greatest thing is to be a master of metaphor. It is the one thing that cannot be learned from others; and it is also an indication of genius, since the ability to forge a good metaphor shows

---

[1] Aeschylus' line means 'This ulcer eats the flesh of my foot'. Euripides substitutes 'feasts upon' for 'eats'.

[2] *Od.* ix. 515.

[3] Homer's line may be rendered 'I that am small, of no account nor goodly'. By the substitution of ordinary words it becomes 'I that am little and weak and ugly'.

[4] *Od.* xx. 259.

[5] Homer's 'Setting a stool unseemly and a table small' becomes 'Setting a shabby stool and a little table'.

[6] 'The sea-shores roar' (*Il.* xvii. 265).

[7] 'The sea-shores croak.'

[8] Perhaps the professional rhapsodist mentioned by Aristophanes.

that the poet has an intuitive perception of the similarity in dissimilars.

Of the kinds of words mentioned in the foregoing pages compounds are best suited to the dithyramb, strange words to heroic, and metaphors to iambic poetry. In heroic poetry indeed all of them are useful instruments. In iambic verse, on the other hand, because it tends to follow the spoken language, only those words are apt which might be used in an oration, i.e. the ordinary word, the metaphor, and the ornamental word.

So much then for Tragedy, the art of imitation by action.

IV. Epic Poetry

As for the poetry which merely narrates, or imitates by means of versified language alone, it clearly has several points in common with Tragedy.

A. Its stories must be constructed in the same way as dramatic plots; they should turn upon a single action, one that is a complete whole in itself, having a beginning, a middle, and an end, so that the work may produce its own proper pleasure with all the organic unity of a living creature. Do not imagine, either, that our usual histories bear any resemblance to them. A history has to give an account not of one action, but of a single period and everything that happened during it to one or more persons, no matter how disconnected the several events may have been. Just as the battle of Salamis and the battle with the Carthaginians in Sicily were simultaneous without converging to the same end,[1] so also of two consecutive events one may occur after the other with no one particular end as their common result. Nevertheless it is fair to say that most epic poets set to work as though they were writing history.

Herein then, as we said earlier on,[2] is a further proof of Homer's overwhelming superiority to the rest. He did not attempt to cover the *whole* Trojan War, notwithstanding the fact that it had a beginning and an end; he doubtless considered it too long a story to be taken in at a

---

[1] Gelo's defeat of the Carthaginians and the Greek victory over the Persians are said by Herodotus to have occurred on the same day in 480 B.C.

[2] Page 17.

single view, or at any rate too complicated from its great variety of incident.   As it is, he has chosen one particular part, but makes use of many other incidents (e.g. the 'Catalogue of Ships', etc.) to diversify his narrative. The other epic poets treat of one man [1459ᵇ] or one period, or in some cases of an action which, although one, has many parts.   This last is the method followed by the authors of *Cypria* and the *Little Iliad*.[1]   The result is that, whereas the *Iliad* and *Odyssey* each afford material for one, or at most two tragedies, the *Cypria* does that for several.   The *Little Iliad* indeed has been the source of more than eight: an *Award of Arms*, a *Philoctetes*, a *Neoptolemus*, a *Eurypylus*, an *Odysseus as Beggar*, a *Laconian Women*, a *Fall of Ilium*, and a *Departure of the Fleet*, not to mention a *Sinon* and a *Trojan Women*.[2]

B. Epic poetry must necessarily include the same species as Tragedy; it must be either simple or complex,[3] a story of character or of suffering.   Its parts also, excluding Song and Spectacle, must be the same, for it too requires Peripeties, Discoveries and scenes of suffering.[4]   Finally its Thought and Diction must be effective.   All these elements appear first in Homer, and he has made adequate use of them.   Each of his two poems are models of construction, the *Iliad* simple and a tale of suffering, the *Odyssey* complex (there is Discovery throughout) and a story of character. Furthermore, they surpass all other poems in Diction and Thought.

---

[1] Lost epics.   The former dealt with the Judgment of Paris and the origin of the Trojan War, the latter with events before Troy following the death of Achilles.

[2] Of these we possess the *Philoctetes* of Sophocles and the *Trojan Women* of Euripides.

[3] *See* page 19.

[4] *See* page 20.

Epic, however, differs from Tragedy in respect of its length and of its metre.

A. As to its length, the limit already suggested [1] will suffice: it must be possible to take in the beginning and the end of the work at a single view, and this will be so if the poem is shorter than the old epics and about as long as the series of tragedies offered at one festival.[2] For the extension of its length epic poetry has a special advantage, of which it makes considerable use. In a tragedy it is impossible to represent an action with a number of parts going on simultaneously; one is limited to the part being acted at a given moment on the stage. In epic poetry, on the other hand, the narrative form enables one to describe a number of simultaneous incidents, whereby (provided they are relevant) the dignity of the poem is increased. This then is a gain to the epic, tending to give it grandeur, to produce a change of mind or mood in the hearer, and to allow room for a variety of episodes. Uniformity soon becomes boring and is apt to ruin tragedies in the theatre.

B. As regards metre, experience has shown the heroic to be most suitable; if anyone wrote a narrative poem in some one, or in several, of the other metres, its incongruity would be apparent. The heroic in fact is the most solemn and weightiest of metres, and for this reason it is particularly capable of digesting strange words and metaphors—another instance of the way in which the narrative form of poetry excels all others. The iambic and trochaic [1460ᵃ] are metres of movement, the former representing that of day-to-day activity, the latter that of the dance. It would be even more out of place if one

---

[1] *See* pages 15–16.
[2] In Aristotle's day this series included nine tragedies and nine satyr plays, amounting in all, perhaps, to about 15,000 or 16,000 lines.

were to write an epic in a medley of metres, like Chaeremon. Consequently no one has ever written a long story in any but heroic verse; nature herself, as we have said, teaches us to choose the metre appropriate to such a story.

Homer, admirable as he is in many other respects, is particularly so in the fact that he alone among epic poets is not unaware of the poet's own function. The poet should say very little *in propria persona*, for he is no imitator when doing that. The other poets are continually expressing their own views and feelings, saying little and infrequently by way of imitation. Homer, on the contrary, after a short prelude, goes on at once to introduce a man, a woman, or some other personage, none of them devoid of character and each with peculiar characteristics.

The marvellous is certainly required in Tragedy. Epic, however, affords more scope for the improbable, the principal ingredient of the marvellous, because one is not actually looking at the agent. The scene of the pursuit of Hector would be ridiculous on the stage, what with the Greeks coming to a halt instead of going after him, and Achilles shaking his head to stop them.[1] The marvellous, however, is a source of pleasure, as appears from the fact that we all tend to embellish a story, in the belief that we are pleasing our hearers.

Homer more than any other has taught the rest of us how to tell lies in the right way. I mean the use of deception caused by a fallacious argument. Whenever, if A is or happens, a consequent, B, is or happens, men think that, if B is or happens, A does so likewise. But that is a false conclusion. Accordingly, if A is *un*true, but there is something else, B, that on the assumption of

[1] *Il*. xx. 205.

A's truth follows as A's consequent, the right thing then is to posit B. Because we know the consequent to be true, our minds are led to the erroneous inference that the antecedent is likewise true. The Bath-story in the *Odyssey* is an example.[1]

A likely impossibility is preferable to an unconvincing possibility. The stories embodied in a poem or play should never consist of improbable incidents. They should contain absolutely nothing of the kind; at the very least such incidents should lie outside the piece, like the hero's ignorance in *Oedipus* of the circumstances of the death of Laius; not within it, like the report of the Pythian games in *Electra*,[2] or the man's having come all the way to Mysia from Tegea without speaking a word on the journey in *The Mysians*.[3]

It is therefore ridiculous to say of a plot that it would have been spoiled without them, since it is fundamentally wrong to construct such plots; and if the poet does take such a plot and could manifestly have given it a more probable form, it will be not only wrong but absurd. Even in the *Odyssey* the improbabilities in the putting ashore of Odysseus [4] would clearly be intolerable [1460b] if an inferior poet were responsible for them. As it is, Homer conceals their absurdity beneath the veil of his other merits. Elaborate diction, however, is required

---

[1] *Od.* xix. 164–260, where Odysseus, disguised as a Cretan and pretending to have entertained Odysseus at Knossos, describes to Penelope her husband's dress, companions, etc. Penelope argues thus: If his story were true he would know all this; but he does; therefore it *is* true.

[2] Sophocles, *Electra*, 660 ff. Aristotle is probably objecting to the anachronism in the reference to the Pythian games.

[3] A lost play probably by Aeschylus. The man referred to was Telephus.

[4] xiii. 116 ff. Odysseus remained fast asleep while the Phaeacians landed him.

only in the parts in which there is no movement and no character or thought to be revealed. Where there is character or thought, on the other hand, an over-ornate diction tends to obscure it.

V. CRITICAL PROBLEMS

As REGARDS problems and their solutions, the number and nature of the assumptions from which they arise will become clear when the subject is viewed as follows. (1) Since the poet is an imitator no less than the painter or other maker of likenesses, he must necessarily in every case represent things in one or other of three aspects, either (a) as they were or are, or (b) as they are said or thought to be or to have been, or (c) as they ought to be. (2) He does this by means of language, with an admixture perhaps of strange words and metaphors, as also of the various modified forms of words, the right to use which we have allowed to the poet. Moreover (3) there is not the same kind of correctness in poetry as in social conduct, or indeed any other art. But poetry itself can go astray in either of two ways—directly or accidentally. If the poet intended to represent a thing correctly, but failed to do so because he lacked power of expression, his work itself is at fault. If, however, it was due to his original conception having been incorrect (e.g. that a moving horse has both right legs thrown forward [1]) that technical errors (e.g. in medicine or some other science) or impossibilities of whatever kind, have crept into his description, his error does not then lie in the essentials of poetic art. These therefore must be the premises of the solutions in answer to criticism involved in the problems.

A. As regards criticisms relative to the poet's art itself. Impossibilities in his descriptions are faults; but all is well if they serve the object of poetry as stated

---

[1] It has, but Aristotle was unaware of the fact.

above,[1] and render the effect of some part of the work more astonishing. The Pursuit of Hector is a case in point. But if that object could have been as well or better attained without this breach of technical exactitude, the impossibility is unjustifiable, since a description should be, if it can, entirely free from error. There is also the question whether the error is in a matter directly or only accidentally connected with the poetic art; for an artist is guilty of a less serious error in being unaware that the hind has no horns than if he produces an unrecognizable picture of one.

B. If the poet's description be criticized on the ground that it is not true to fact, one may perhaps retort that the object *ought* to be as described—an answer like that of Sophocles, who said that he depicted men as they ought to be, and Euripides as they actually were. If the description, however, is true neither to fact nor of the thing as it ought to be, the defence may then argue that it accords with tradition. Stories about gods, for instance, may be wrong as Xenophanes thinks, neither true nor the better thing to say;[2] but they are certainly in line with tradition. [1461ᵃ] In other cases one may perhaps urge not that the statement is better than the truth, but that the fact was so at the time to which it refers. Take, for example, Homer's description of the arms: 'Their spears stood upright, butt-end on the ground'.[3] That was the usual way of piling them in those days, as it still is with the Illyrians. As for the question whether something said or done in a poem is morally right or wrong, one should consider not only the word or deed in itself, but also the person who says or does it, the person to whom he

[1] Page 48.

[2] Xenophanes' criticism was directed at Homer's anthropomorphic religion and the immoral behaviour of the gods.

[3] *Il.* x. 152. The criticism is that it seems a bad way to pile arms, because they might collapse at night and cause an alarm.

says or does it, the time, the means, and the motive of the agent—whether he does it to attain a greater good, or to avoid a greater evil.

C. Other criticisms must be met by a consideration of the poet's language: (1) by the assumption of a strange word, e.g. in Homer's phrase *ourēas men prōton*,[1] where *ourēas* may possibly mean not mules but sentinels. And in saying of Dolon, *hos rh' ē toi eidos men eēn kakos*,[2] he may mean not that Dolon's body was deformed,[3] but that he had an ugly face, as *eueidēs* is the Cretan word for handsome-faced. So too *zōroteron de keraie*[4] may mean not 'mix the wine stronger', as though for topers, but 'mix it quicker'. (2) Other Homeric expressions may be explained as metaphorical; e.g. in *alloi men rha theoi te kai aneres heudon . . . hapantes pannukhioi*, as compared with what he says at the same time, *ē toi hot' es pedion to Trōikon athrēseien, aulōn suringōn th' omadon*, the word *hapantes* ('all') is used metaphorically for 'many', since 'all' is a species of 'many'.[5] His *oiē d' ammoros* is likewise metaphorical,[6] the best known standing alone. (3) As Hippias of Thasos suggested, a change in the mode of

---

[1] *Il.* i. 50: 'The mules first [and swift-footed hounds he (Apollo) first beset with his arrows]'. Zoilus, a fierce critic of Homer, described mules as 'small deer for a deity'.

[2] *Il.* x. 316: 'One who was very evil in form, [but swift in his running]'.

[3] In which case he can hardly have been a good runner.

[4] *Il.* ix. 202: 'Livelier mix it'.

[5] The first of these excerpts (*Il.* ii. 1, 2, quoted in error for x. 1, 2) means 'the other gods and all the . . . men slept all night long'. The second means 'Yea when indeed [Agamemnon] gazed on the Trojan plain [he marvelled at voices] of flutes and of pipes [and the din of the soldiers]'. If *all* were asleep, whence all the noise?

[6] *Il.* xviii. 489 says of the Great Bear: 'She alone shares not [in the baths of Ocean]', i.e. never sets. But there are other constellations that never do so. Consequently 'alone' must be used of the Great Bear as meaning 'best known', which is a species of 'alone'.

reading a word will solve the difficulty in *didomen de hoi*, and *to men ou kataputhetai ombrō*.[1] (4) Other difficulties may be solved by a change of punctuation, e.g. in Empedocles: *aipsa de thnēt' ephuonto, ta prin mathon athanata zw̄ra te prin kekrēto*.[2] Or (5) by the assumption of an equivocal term, as in *parōikhēken de pleō nux*,[3] where *pleō* is equivocal. Or (6) by an appeal to linguistic usage. In common parlance a mixture of wine and water is said to be 'wine'; and on the same principle Homer has written of a 'greave of new-wrought tin'.[4] We describe a worker in iron as a 'brazier'; and on the same principle Ganymede is said to 'serve Zeus with wine' even though the gods do not drink wine. But this latter expression may be metaphorical.[5] Nevertheless whenever a word seems to indicate some contradiction, one must take account of the fact that it may have more than one meaning in the passage under review; e.g. in *tē rh' eskheto khalkeon engkhos* [6] one must consider the possible senses

[1] The first quotation is from the beginning of *Il.* ii, though different from the reading of our text. If the first word is written *didomen* it means 'We grant him', and makes Zeus tell a lie. But change the accent, *didómen*, and it means 'Grant thou him', and the Dream becomes the liar. The second quotation is from *Il.* xxiii. 327: 'A fathom high from the earth rises a withered stump . . . that does not rot in the rain'. This seems highly unlikely; so for *ou* read *hou*, and the meaning becomes '. . . part of it rots in the rain'.

[2] 'Soon they [elements or atoms] grew mortal that erstwhile learnt mortal ways, and pure erstwhile commingled'. As the words stand they can either mean that those which were erstwhile pure commingled, or that those became pure which were erstwhile commingled. Only the reader's pause or punctuation will show which.

[3] *Il.* x. 253. '*More* than two parts of the night are gone [but a third remains]'. This is impossible; but *pleō* may mean 'fully'.

[4] Greaves were in fact made of bronze, a mixture of copper and tin.

[5] Aristotle means that nectar, the drink of gods, may stand in relation to them as wine does to men.

[6] *Il.* xx. 272. The armour of Achilles consisted of five layers: one of gold, two of bronze, and the innermost two of tin. According

of 'was stopped there'—whether by interpreting it in this way or in that we shall best avoid the fault [1461ᵇ] of which Glaucon speaks: 'They start with an improbable assumption; and having thus decreed it themselves, proceed to draw inferences and condemn the poet as though he had said whatever they happen to think he has said, if his statement is at variance with their own idea of things'. This is how Homer's silence about Icarius has been treated.[1] Taking their stand on the assumption that he must have been a Spartan, the critics think it unlikely that Telemachus did not meet him when he visited Sparta. But it is quite likely, as the Cephalenian say, that Odysseus' wife belonged to a Cephalenian family, and that his name was Icadius, not Icarius. It is therefore probably a mistake on the part of the critics that has given rise to the difficulty.

Generally speaking, one has to justify (1) the impossible by reference to the demands of poetry, or to idealization, or to opinion. For the purposes of poetry a convincing impossibility is preferable to an unconvincing possibility; and if men such as Zeuxis depicted the impossible, the answer is it is better they should be like that, since an artist should always improve on his model. (2) One has to justify the improbable by showing either (a) that the statement criticized has the sanction of opinion, or (b) that the incident which it describes was not so improbable, bearing in mind the time when it is said to have occurred; for there is a probability of things happening

---

to Homer the spear thrown by Aeneas 'penetrated two layers and was stopped in the gold'. The gold must obviously have been outermost, which raises the question of how the spear could first have penetrated two layers. The answer may be that although the point of the spear drove through the two layers of bronze, it was the gold on the surface that actually 'stopped it' by slowing down its speed.

[1] See *Od.* IV. I.

also against probability. (3) As regards contradictions in the language [1] of a poet, one should first test them as one does an opponent's confutation in a dialectical argument, to see whether he means the same thing, in the same relation and in the same sense, before declaring that he has contradicted either something he has said himself or what an ordinary intelligent man assumes to be true. There is, on the other hand, no excuse for improbability of plot or depravity of character [2] when they are not necessary and no use is made of them, e.g. the unlikely appearance of Aegeus in Euripides' *Medea* and the baseness of Menelaus in his *Orestes*.

Critical objections are thus of five kinds: they allege that something impossible, improbable, corrupting, contradictory, or technically incorrect. The answers to them, which are twelve in number, must be sought under one or other of the above-mentioned heads.

[1] As distinct from the matter.
[2] Only such faults of character may be depicted as are necessary for the outcome of the plot.

VI. Comparative Value of Tragic and Epic Poetry

THE question may be raised whether the epic or the tragic is the higher form of imitation. It may be urged that if the less vulgar is the higher, and the less vulgar is always that which appeals to the better public, an art which makes its appeal to all and sundry is clearly one of a very low order indeed. The argument is that because the poet's public cannot grasp the meaning of a piece unless the author adds something, he is led to keep the performers in perpetual motion—have flute players, for example, rolling about if the act of throwing a quoit is to be imitated, and pulling at the conductor if the music is descriptive of Scylla. Tragedy then is said to be an art of this sort, to be in fact just what the later actors were in the eyes of their predecessors; for Mynniscus used to call Callipides 'the ape' because he thought his style was exaggerated, and a similar view [1462a] was taken of Pindarus also.[1] All Tragedy, however, is said to stand to Epic as the later to the older school of actors. The one is accordingly said to address a cultured audience, which has no need of gesture as an accompaniment; the other, an uncultured one. If therefore Tragedy is a vulgar art, it must clearly be lower than Epic.

We may answer this in the first place by urging (1) that the censure is not directed at the art of the dramatic poet but at that of the man who interprets him; for it is possible to overdo the gesturing even in an epic recital, as

[1] Nothing is known of Pindarus. Mynniscus acted for Aeschylus; Callipides was his younger contemporary.

did Sosistratus, and in a singing contest, as did Mnasi-
theus of Opus. We may urge (2) that all movement
should not be condemned, unless the very dance itself is
to be condemned also, but only that of ignoble persons;
that indeed is the point of the criticism directed at
Callippides, and nowadays at others as well, that their
women are not like gentlewomen. We may urge (3)
that Tragedy may produce its effect without movement
or action in the same way as Epic; for the quality of a
play can be discovered by merely reading it. Consequently if it is superior in all other respects this element
of inferiority is no intrinsic part of it.

In the second place we must bear in mind four things.
(1) Tragedy has everything that Epic has (even the epic
metre being admissible), and also the not inconsiderable
addition of the music (a very real factor in the pleasure
afforded by drama) and the spectacle. (2) Its reality is
conveyed through reading no less than through presenta-
tion on the stage. (3) [1462^b] Tragic imitation requires
less space for the attainment of its end; and this is an
advantage since the more concentrated effect is more
pleasurable than one with a large admixture of time, as
may be seen from considering Sophocles' *Oedipus* and
the effect of expanding it into a poem as long as the *Iliad*.
(4) Imitation as practised by the epic poets has less unity,
as is clear from the fact that any one work of theirs
provides material for several tragedies; the result being
that if they write what is really a single story, it seems
curt when briefly narrated, and thin and watery when on
the scale of length usual with their verse. When I say
that an epic has less unity, I refer to one made up of a
plurality of actions, like the *Iliad* and *Odyssey*, which
have many parts, each of some magnitude; yet the structure of these two works is as perfect as could possibly be,
and the action in them is as nearly as possible one action.

If then Tragedy is superior in these respects—and also in its emotional effect, since the two forms of poetry should create not any random kind of pleasure, but the special kind we have mentioned—it will clearly be the higher form of art as attaining the emotional effect better than Epic.

So much for Tragedy and Epic poetry, both in general and in their several species; the number and nature of their constituent parts; the causes of their success or failure; the objections of critics and the means of answering them.

APPENDIX

I. The Quantitative Division of Tragedy
[1452ᵇ14–27]

See page 21, footnote 2

I MENTIONED on an earlier occasion [1] the parts of Tragedy to be treated as its constituent elements. From the point of view of its quantity, i.e. the several sections into which it is divided, a tragedy has the following parts: Prologue, Episode, Exode, and a choral section. This last is made up of Parode and Stasimon, which are common to all tragedies, whereas songs from the stage and *kommoi* are found only in some.

The prologue is all that precedes the parode of the chorus; an episode, all that lies between two choral songs; the exode, all that follows the last choral song. In the choral section the parode is the entire first utterance of the chorus; a stasimon, a song of the chorus without anapaestic or trochaic lines. [2]

---

[1] Page 12.

[2] Aristotle is probably referring here to the tragedies of his own day, as his statement about the anapaests and trochees is not true of the tragedies that have come down to us. The parode was sung as the chorus entered the orchestra; stasima, after it had taken up its position. The last three lines of the section are omitted here; they are an almost verbatim repetition of the opening sentence.

II. A GRAMMATICAL NOTE ON DICTION
[1456ᵇ20–57ᵃ30]

See page 35, footnote 1

THE parts of Diction considered as a whole are as follows: the Letter, the Syllable, the Conjunction, the Article, the Noun, the Verb, the Mode, and the Speech.

1. The Letter is an indivisible sound, not any and every kind of sound, but one that may become a constituent element of a word. Brute beasts also utter indivisible sounds, but none of the latter is a letter according to my definition. These elementary sounds are classified as vowels, semi-vowels, and mutes. A vowel is a letter having an audible sound without the addition of another letter; a semi-vowel (e.g. S and R), one having an audible sound by the addition of another letter; a mute (e.g. D and G), one having no sound at all by itself but becoming audible by the addition of one of the letters which have some sound of their own. The letters differ (*a*) as produced by different conformations or in different regions of the mouth; (*b*) as aspirated, not aspirated, or sometimes one and sometimes the other; (*c*) as long, short, or of variable quantity; (*d*) as having an acute, grave, or circumflex accent. To study the details of these matters is the business of metricians.

2. The Syllable is a non-significant composite sound, made up of a mute and a vowel or semi-vowel; for GR *without* an A is no less a syllable than GRA, *with* an A. The several forms of the syllable also belong to the theory of metre.

3. A Conjunction is (*a*) a non-significant sound which, [1457ᵃ] when one significant sound is formable out of several, neither hinders nor helps the union, and which, if the speech thus formed stands by itself, must not be

inserted at the beginning of it; e.g. *men, dē, toi, de.* Or
(*b*) it is a non-significant sound capable of combining
two or more significant sounds into one; e.g. *amphi,
peri,* etc.

4. An Article is a non-significant sound that marks the
beginning, end, or dividing point of a speech, its natural
place being at the extremities or in the middle.[1]

5. A Noun [2] is a composite significant sound which
does not involve the idea of time and whose parts have no
significance by themselves in it. In a compound, you
see, we do not treat the parts as having significance also
by themselves; the word *dōron* (gift) implied in the name
'Theodorus' means nothing to us.

6. A Verb is a composite significant sound involving
the idea of time and having parts which (just as in the
Noun) have no significance by themselves in it. Whereas
the word 'man' or 'white' does not indicate *when,*
'walks' and 'has walked' involve in addition to the idea
of walking that of present and past time.

7. The mode includes (*a*) the oblique cases of all nouns,
as compared with the nominative (e.g. when the word
means 'of' or 'to' a thing, etc.); (*b*) the nominative of
common nouns, as suggesting number (e.g. 'man' and
'men'); or (*c*) it may consist in the mode of utterance of a
verb, e.g. in question, command, etc. ('Walked?' and
'Walk!' are modes of the verb 'to walk').

8. A Speech is a composite significant sound, some of
whose parts have a certain significance all on their own.[3]

[1] Those marking the beginning are, probably, conditional and
causal conjunctions, relative pronouns and adverbs; those
marking the end, final and illative conjunctions; those marking
the dividing point, disjunctives.

[2] *See* page 35, note 2.

[3] A speech does not always consist of noun and verb; it may be
without a verb, like the definition of man; but it will always have
some part with a certain significance by itself.—(A.)

Thus in the speech 'Cleon walks', Cleon is such a part. A speech has unity in one of two ways, either as signifying one thing, or as consisting of several speeches forged into one by conjunction. The *Iliad*, for example, is one speech by conjunction of several, while the definition of man is one by virtue of its signifying one thing.

DEMETRIUS ON STYLE

TRANSLATED BY T. A. MOXON

I

(1) As poetry is distinguished by metres, for example, the half-measure or the hexameter and so forth, so prose style is distinguished by what we call 'members'.[1] These 'members' might be said to give a rest to the speaker and his subject matter; they set constant bounds to his discourse; otherwise it would be tedious and boundless and would render him completely breathless.

(2) The function of these members is to mark the completion of an idea. Sometimes a member marks an idea as complete in itself, as, for example, when Hecataeus says at the beginning of his history: 'Hecataeus of Miletus relates what follows'. A complete idea is comprised in a complete member; the two begin and end together. Sometimes a member does not comprehend a complete idea, but only a part of it, which is, however, complete in itself. As the arm is complete, and yet certain portions of it are also complete, for example, the fingers and forearm (for each of these parts has its own bounds and its own component parts), so a long idea, though complete, may contain a number of parts which are also complete themselves.

(3) For example, at the beginning of Xenophon's *Anabasis* the following instance appears: 'Darius and Parysatis' down to the words 'but the younger was Cyrus' is all one idea. But its two members are each a

---

[1] 'Members', i.e. 'limbs'; here 'clauses', whether they are short sentences or subdivisions of a complete sentence.

part of it, and each of them comprises an idea which is complete in itself. First 'Darius and Parysatis had sons'. The idea contained in this has a completeness of its own, namely, that sons were born to Darius and Parysatis. The same fact applies to the second member that 'the elder was Artaxerxes and the younger Cyrus'. The member, therefore, as I maintain, will comprise an idea which is either complete in itself or an essential part of a complete sentence.

(4) The members ought not to be made very long; in that case, the composition is lacking in symmetry or hard to follow. Even poetry does not exceed the measure of six feet, except on rare occasions. It is absurd that the metre should lack symmetry, and that when it ends we should forget when it began. Long members, then, are unfitting in prose because they lack symmetry, and short members are unfitting, as in that case the composition would be described as 'arid'. The following example is an illustration: 'Life is short; art is long; time is fleeting'. The composition seems curtailed and whittled down and unimpressive, because its component parts are brief.

(5) Sometimes a long member is not actually out of place; for example in sublime passages, as in the passage of Plato: 'As for this universe as a whole, God Himself in His course guides it and helps to make it revolve on its way'. The very language corresponds to the sublimity of the member. That is why the hexameter is called a heroic metre because of its length, and is suited to the story of heroes. Homer's Iliad would not be written fittingly in the brief measure of Archilochus; for example:

'Grief-stricken staff',

'Who led thy mind astray?'

nor in the measure of Anacreon; for example:

'Bring me drink, bring wine, my page-boy'.

Such a rhythm would be quite appropriate to a drunken old man, but not to a hero engaged in battle.

(6) A long member might sometimes be appropriate, for the reasons mentioned. A short member might also be appropriate, as, for example, when our subject is small. Xenophon, in his description of the arrival of the Greeks at the river Teleboas, says: 'This river was not great, but was beautiful'. The slightness and beauty of the river harmonized with the slightness and abruptness of the rhythm. If he had extended the idea thus: 'This river fell short of the majority of rivers in size, but exceeded all in beauty', he would have failed in taste, and have been what is called 'frigid'. We must, however, speak about the frigid style later.

(7) Short members may also be used in a forceful style. A great idea comprised in a small compass is more forceful and vigorous. The Lacedemonians, therefore, are sparing of words because of their forcefulness. A command is concise and brief, and every master uses few words to a slave; but supplication and lamentation are lengthy. The Prayers are described in Homer as lame and wrinkled because of their slowness, that is their lengthiness, and old men are described as garrulous through weakness.

(8) An example of brevity in composition is seen in the message of the Lacedemonians to Philip: 'Dionysius in Corinth'. The message appears much more forceful when thus briefly stated than if they had spoken at length and said: 'Dionysius, who was once a great tyrant like yourself, now is living as a private citizen in Corinth'. When stated at length it resembles not a protest but a narrative; it suggests information, not intimidation.

Thus a spirited and vehement expression by being expanded is weakened. As wild beasts gather their limbs together for an attack, so language also should gather itself as it were into a coil to acquire force.

(9) Such brevity in composition is called a 'clause'. Clauses are defined as follows: 'A clause is that which is less than a member'; for example, the words already quoted, 'Dionysius in Corinth'; or the maxims of sages: 'Know thyself', and 'Follow God'. Brevity is suitable to apophthegms and proverbs, and the contraction of a large idea into a small compass is a sign of superior wisdom, just as whole trees exist potentially in seeds. If a proverb were expanded, it would savour of instruction and rhetoric and be no more a proverb.

(10) From a combination of members and clauses such as these are formed what are called 'periods'. A period is a combination of members or clauses fitted together exactly to express the underlying idea; for example: 'First because I thought it expedient for the State that the law should be cancelled, and secondly, for the sake of Chabrias' son, I complied with my clients' wish to plead their case to the best of my powers'. This period, which consists of three members, has a turning point and a concentration which keeps the end in view.

(11) Aristotle's definition of the period is as follows: 'A period is a mode of expression which has a beginning and an end'. This definition is good and appropriate. The term 'period' indicates that it began at a certain point and will finish at a certain point, and is hastening towards a definite goal, like runners who have started their race. In their case the goal is evident directly they begin to run. Hence comes the term 'period', which is compared to journeys which are circular and move in an orbit. To speak generally, a period is

nothing but a certain combination of words. At any rate, if its circular form were removed and the order were changed, the subject-matter would remain unchanged, but the period would vanish. If, for example, you upset the period of Demosthenes which has been quoted, and paraphrase it thus: 'I will support my clients, Athenians; Chabrias' son is dear to me; still more dear is the City, and it is only right for me to support it', the period ceases to exist any more.

(12) I will now describe the origin of the period. One kind of style is described as 'connected', as, for example, the style which is expressed by periods. It is seen in the style of the speeches of Isocrates and Gorgias and Alcidamas. These speeches are expressed as completely by the medium of periods as Homer's poetry is by the medium of hexameters. The other style is called 'disconnected', and is resolved into members which are not clearly related, as, for example, the style of Hecataeus and the greater part of Herodotus, and all ancient writers in general. Here is an illustration: 'Hecataeus of Miletus tells his story thus. The events I describe are, as I think, true. The stories told by the Greeks appear to me to be numerous and ridiculous'. The members here seem to be flung upon one another in a heap and cast at random. They have neither connection nor mutual support nor do they help one another, like the members in periods.

(13) The members of periods are like stones which support and uphold vaulted ceilings; periods in the loose style are like stones which are merely flung in a heap and not fitted together.

(14) Therefore the style of the ancients possesses a quality of polish and compactness, like the early statues, the art of which seemed to consist of simplicity and plainness. The style of the later writers seems to

resemble the works of Pheidias, and possesses a combination of sublimity and accuracy.

(15) I think that speech should neither consist wholly of a string of periods, like that of Gorgias, nor be wholly disconnected like that of the ancients, but should possess a combination of both qualities. Thus it will blend elaborateness with simplicity, and by this combination it will be pleasing, being neither too untrained nor too artificial. When men produce a series of periods, their heads begin to reel like drunken men, and their hearers are sickened by the unconvincing style; and then they anticipate the conclusions of the periods, and bawl them out before the speaker.

(16) Smaller periods consist of two members: the largest consist of four. Anything that exceeds four would go beyond the scope of the symmetry of a period.

(17) Some periods have three members; some have only one, and these are called 'simple periods'. When the member has length and is rounded off at the end, then it becomes a period with one member, as for example: 'The following is the result of the inquiry of Herodotus of Halicarnassus', or again: 'Lucid utterance throws a flood of light on the minds of hearers'. The simple period possesses two properties, length and its final rounding. Without either of these it is not a period.

(18) In composite periods the last member should be longer than the others, and should, as it were, contain and include them all. Thus the period will be stately and impressive, ending with an impressive and long member. Otherwise it will seem abrupt and halting. The following is an example of this: 'Nobility consists not in noble words, but in speaking first and then in translating one's words into action.'

(19) There are three kinds of periods, which belong to history, dialogue, and rhetoric. The historical

period is neither too artificial nor too careless, but a blend between the two. It must not appear rhetorical and unconvincing because of its artificial style, but be impressive and straightforward by reason of its simplicity: as in the passage 'Darius and Parysatis' down to the words, 'but the younger was Cyrus'. The pause in the period suggests a stable and sure conclusion.

(20) The rhetorical period has a compact and well-rounded form; it requires a terse utterance, and a gesture that harmonizes with the rhythm. For example: 'First because I thought it expedient for the State that the law should be cancelled, and secondly, for the sake of Chabrias' son, I complied with my clients' wish to plead their case to the best of my power'. From the very opening such a period has something compact about it, something which shows that it will not finish tamely.

(21) The period of dialogue is one which is as yet unformed, and simpler than that of history. It hardly reveals the fact that it is a period. For example: 'I went down yesterday to the Peiraeus', down to the words, 'since they were now celebrating it for the first time'. The members are flung at random one on another, as though the style were loose. On reaching the end, we scarcely realize that the passage was a period. The period of dialogue must be midway between the 'disconnected' and 'connected' style and possess elements belonging to both. Such are the various kinds of periods.

(22) Periods are also found of antithetical members, which are either antithetical in matter, as, for example: 'Sailing over the mainland and marching over the sea', or both in language and in matter, of which the same period is an instance.

(23) There are also periods antithetical in words

alone, as in the contrast between Helen and Heracles: 'The life of the one he filled with toil and hazard; the form of the other he rendered an object of admiration and contention'. These sentences are contrasted, article to article, conjunction to conjunction, and like to like; in fact, the whole sentence is one long antithesis. 'Filled' and 'rendered', 'toil' and 'admiration', 'hazard' and 'contention', are all opposed to each other, point to point, and like to like.

(24) There are members which, though not antithetical, give an appearance of antithesis because of their antithetical form. There is for example, the playful passage in the poet Epicharmus: 'At one time I was among them; at another time I was with them'. The same idea is repeated without any change; but the form of the sentence which imitates antithesis appears to mislead. He perhaps adopted this form in a humorous manner and to poke fun at rhetoricians.

(25) Members are sometimes closely similar; this similarity may be at the beginning, as, for example: 'Open to bribes they were and open to prayers uttered in words'. It may be at the end of the clause, as is seen in the opening words of the *Panegyric*: 'I have often wondered at the men who convened the assemblies and instituted the games'. The similarity may take the form of equality of members, when the members contain an equal number of syllables, as in Thucydides: 'Those who are asked do not disown the work; and those who inquire do not censure the task'. This passage shows an equality of members.

(26) The homoeoteleuton is used when sentences end in a similar way. They may end with identical words, as in the passage: 'In his lifetime you spoke of him disparagingly; now after his death you write of him disparagingly'. They may, again, end with the same

syllable, as in the passage already quoted from the *Panegyric*.

(27) The use of such members is beset with danger. Such a device is unsuitable to a forceful speaker. The artifice and elaboration spoils the vigour. Theopompos makes this clear to us. In accusing the friends of Philip, he says: 'Men-slayers they were by nature, and men-defilers by habit. They were called companions; they were really courtesans'. The balance and antithesis of the members spoils the vigour through ill-applied artifice. Indignation does not require artifice; the style should be natural in such denunciations, and the words should be simple.

(28) Such a device is useless in a forceful passage, as I have shown; it is also useless in passionate argument and in character-sketches. Passion and character-study are essentially simple and natural. In Aristotle's treatise *On Justice* someone was bewailing the fate of Athens. If the speaker were to say: 'What city did I ever capture from my enemies as great as my own city which they destroyed?' he would have spoken with tragedy and pathos. If, however, he balances his clauses and says: 'What city of my foes have I won, like to my own which is undone?', believe me he will excite neither pathos nor pity, but only what is called 'laughter with tears'. To misapply artifice in this way in a pathetic passage is like the proverbial 'jest in a house of mourning'.

(29) The device is, however, useful on certain occasions as in the passage of Aristotle: 'I came from Athens to Stageira because of the great king, and from Stageira to Athens because of the great storm'. If you remove the second 'great' you will at once lose the charm of the passage. Such members help to make the sentence impressive, as do also the many antithetical passages

of Gorgias and Isocrates. This will do, then, for similarity of language.

(30) An enthymeme differs from a period, because the period is a rounded composition, whence it derives its name, while the enthymeme contains its force and cohesion in the sense. The period comprehends the enthymeme, as also it comprehends all other subject-matter, but the enthymeme is an idea expressed either controversially or as a logical sequence.

(31) The following is an illustration. If you resolve the structure of the enthymeme, you destroy the period, but the enthymeme remains intact. If, for example, you were to resolve the following enthymeme of Demosthenes: 'Had one of them been convicted, you would not have made these proposals. If, therefore, you are now convicted, no one else will make such proposals'— if you resolve it thus: 'Make no allowance for those who make unconstitutional proposals. If they were continuously checked, the defendant would not now be making these proposals. And in the future no one else will do so if he is now convicted'; you discard the circular form of the period, but the enthymeme remains unchanged.

(32) To speak generally, an enthymeme is a syllogism in a rhetorical form; but a period is not a syllogism, it is a mere combination of words. Periods are found in every form of composition, for example, in introductions. Enthymemes are not found everywhere. The enthymeme is, as it were, an appendage, but the period is found anywhere. The enthymeme is an informal syllogism, but the period has no syllogistic character, whether formal or informal.

(33) The enthymeme, then, happens also to be a period, because its structure is that of a period; but a period is not an enthymeme. For example, a building happens

to be white if that is its colour; but whiteness is not an essential characteristic of a building. This, then, will suffice for the difference between an enthymeme and a period.

(34) Aristotle defines a member thus: 'A member is one of the two parts of a period'. He then adds the rider: 'A period is sometimes simple'. By using the phrase 'one of the two parts' in his definition, he clearly wishes to confine a period to two members. Archedemus combined the definition of Aristotle and its rider and produced a clearer and more perfect definition: 'A member is either a simple period or a part of a composite period'.

(35) A simple period has already been described. When he says that a member is part of a composite period, it is clear that he is not confining the period to two members, but will admit three or even more. I have treated of the measure of a period; and now ask leave to speak of the kinds of style.

II

(36) The simple kinds of style are four: 'plain', 'stately', 'polished', and 'powerful'; there are also those which combine these characteristics. They are not combined indiscriminately, but the 'polished' is combined with the 'plain' and the 'stately'; the 'powerful' style with both alike. The plain and stately alone will not combine, but they are the opposites and contraries of one another. For this reason some maintain that these are the only two kinds of style, and that the rest lie midway between them; they regard the polished as nearer to the plain, and the powerful as nearer to the stately; they maintain that the polished

style contains something slight and smart, while the powerful style contains something massive and great.

(37) Such an argument is absurd. Apart from the opposite kinds of style mentioned, we see all mingled together. For example, the epic verse of Homer and the prose of Plato and Xenophon and Herodotus and many other writers combine much stateliness with much power and grace. The number of kinds, then, will be such as I have described. Each one, however, will have an appropriate diction somewhat as follows.

(38) I will begin with stately style, which is now called erudite. Stateliness requires three qualities: idea, expression, and suitable composition. Aristotle tells us that the paeonian rhythm produces a stately diction. The paeon has two forms; the one begins a sentence and its first syllable is long, and it ends with three short syllables, as, for example, 'prīmărĭly̆'. The closing paeon is opposite to the other, and it begins with three short syllables and ends with one long syllable, for example, Ărăbĭā.

(39) In the stately style, the members should begin with the opening paeon and the closing paeon should follow. The following passage of Thucydides will serve as an example:

$$\bar{\eta}\rho\xi\breve{a}\tau\breve{o}\ \delta\breve{\epsilon}\ \tau\breve{o}\ \kappa\breve{a}\kappa\breve{o}\nu\ \bar{\epsilon}\xi\ \text{'}A\iota\theta\iota\breve{o}\pi\acute{\iota}\bar{a}\varsigma.$$

Why, then, did Aristotle advise this arrangement of syllables? It is because the member must have a stately opening and a stately ending. This will be so if we begin on a long syllable and end on a long syllable. Long syllables tend naturally to be stately. A long syllable at the beginning produces an explosive effect, and at the end it leaves the hearer on a stately note. At any rate, we all remember the opening and closing words particularly and are moved by them. This applies in a less degree to the middle words which are, as it were, concealed and unobtrusive.

(40) This fact can be seen in Thucydides. Throughout it is almost always the long syllables in his rhythm that create his stately diction. It may be said that this arrangement of words is the chief, if not the only factor, in producing the stateliness of language which prevails in his writings.

(41) We must however realize that even if we cannot actually place the two kinds of paeon one at each end of the members, we shall be able at any rate to invest our composition with a paeonic character, as, for example, by beginning with long syllables and ending with long syllables. This is what Aristotle actually seems to recommend, though for the sake of precision he has defined the two kinds of paeon. So Theophrastus put forward the following member as an example of the stately style:

τῶν μὲν περὶ τὰ μηδενὸς ἄξια φιλοσοφούντων.

This does not actually consist of paeons, but it has a paeonic character. The paeon, however, should be introduced into prose, as it is a mixed rhythm and safer; it derives its stateliness from the long syllable, and its prose character from the short syllables.

(42) Of other metres, the heroic is solemn and unsuitable for prose. It is sonorous and unrhythmical, as the following quotation shows:

ἥκων ἡμῶν εἰς τὴν χώραν.

The repetition of long syllables goes beyond the prose rhythm.

(43) The iambic is a weak metre and resembles ordinary conversation. At any rate, people often talk unconsciously in iambics. But the paeon strikes the

happy mean between the two and is, as it were, compounded of both. The paeonic rhythm may thus be
adopted in stately passages.

(44) The length of members also creates grandeur,
as in the passages: 'Thucydides, an Athenian,
wrote the history of the war between the Pelopon-
nesians and the Athenians,' and 'Herodotus of
Halicarnassus thus gives the result of his inquiries.'
Suddenly to pause on a short member diminishes the
impressiveness of the passage, even though the underlying sentiment or the actual words be stately.

(45) Stateliness is also produced by adopting a
rounded period, as is seen in Thucydides: 'The river
Achelous, which flows from Mount Pindus through
Dolopia and the land of the Agrianians and Amphi-
lochians, and passes by the town Stratos and discharges
into the sea close to Oeniadae, and surrounds the town
with a marsh, makes it impossible to land an army
against it in winter, because of the water.' The whole
of the stateliness of this passage is due to its rounded
period, and to the fact that it scarcely allows a pause
either to the writer or to the reader.

(46) If you were to break up the passage and write
it thus: 'The river Achelous flows from Mount Pindus.
It discharges into the sea at Oeniadae. Before it
empties, it makes a marsh of the plains of Oeniadae,
with the result that the water forms a protection and
defence against attacks of the enemy in winter'—if you
were to paraphrase the passage thus, you would have
many resting places in the narrative, but you would
rob it of its impressiveness.

(47) As frequent inns make long journeys short, and
lonely paths give an impression of length even on short
roads, so the same effect can be seen in periods.

(48) Often roughness of composition produces stateli-

ness; for example: 'Ajax the mighty always was aiming at Hector the bronze-helmeted'. It is true that the collision of letters is harsh to the ear, but still the very excess emphasizes the greatness of the hero. Smoothness and softness of sound have not much place in stately diction, except on rare occasions. Thucydides everywhere avoids smoothness and evenness of composition. He always resembles a man who is stumbling, like those who tread rugged paths, when, for example, he says: 'The year, as was agreed, happened to be free from disease, so far as all other maladies were concerned'. It could have been expressed more easily and more pleasantly as follows, that 'the year was free from disease, in respect of other maladies', but it would have lost its stately character.

(49) As a rough word produces an impressive effect, so does the arrangement of the words. Instances of rough words are 'bawling' for 'shouting', and 'bursting' for 'moving'. Thucydides uses all these, approximating his language to his composition, and his composition to his language.

(50) Words should be arranged thus. First should come those words that are not very brilliant, second and last the more brilliant words. In this way we shall hear the first word with an idea of brilliance, and what which follows as more brilliant still. Otherwise we shall seem to have become tame, and, as it were, to have fallen from strength to weakness.

(51) An example is found in Plato: 'When you allow any one to play music and to flood your soul through your ears'. The second phrase is far more arresting than the former. Again, he says later: 'When he never ceases to flood your soul with it, but charms you like a serpent, he then causes it to melt and waste away'. The words 'melt' and 'waste away' are more expressive

and more like poetry. If he had reversed the order, the word 'melt' would have appeared weaker, coming afterwards.

(52) Homer, too, in the Cyclops passage, continually heightens his expression and seems to mount up, rung by rung, as for example: 'For he was not like to any man that lives by bread, but like a wooded peak', and the further phrase, 'or towering hill', and 'standing out above other hills'. The former words, impressive though they are, seem less and less important, as those which follow them are more impressive still.

(53) The connective particles should not correspond exactly; for example, the particles μέν and δέ. Such exactness is unimpressive. They should be used with a certain measure of looseness, as Antiphon somewhere says: 'The island (μέν) which we own, is easily seen (μέν) even from a distance, for it is lofty and rugged. The parts of it which are useful (μέν) and arable are small; but its uncultivated (δέ) parts are many, in spite of its small size'. The particle μέν occurs three times, and is followed by a single δέ.

(54) It often happens, however, that connectives which follow in close succession make even small things great, as in Homer the names of Boeotian cities, trivial and unimportant though they are, acquire a majesty and a stateliness through a close succession of conjunctions, as in the passage: 'Both Schoinos and Scolos and deep-spurred Eteonos'.

(55) Expletive particles must not be used as empty appendages, and as mere additions or excrescences, as people are apt to use the particles δή and νυ and πρότερον, in a pointless way—but only if they contribute something to the stateliness of the passage.

(56) So in Plato: 'Lo (μὲν δή) mighty Zeus in heaven', and in Homer: 'But when (δή) at last they reached the

ford of the fair-flowing stream'. The particle placed at
the beginning and separating what follows from what
precedes produces a stately effect. To amplify the
beginning produces something impressive. If he had
merely said, 'When they reached the ford of the river',
he would have seemed unimpressive, as though he were
simply describing a single incident.

(57) This particle is also employed often in pathetic
passages, as in the passage when Calypso says to
Odysseus: 'Son of Laertes, of the seed of Zeus, Odysseus
of many devices, so is it indeed (δή) thy wish to get thee
home to thine own dear country'. If you remove the
particle, you will remove the pathos also. To sum
up, as Praxiphanes says, these particles were employed instead of lamentations and groans, such as 'ah
me!' and 'alas!' and 'what is this!'. As he himself
says, the words καί νύ κε were appropriate to those
uttering lamentations, and they suggest the idea of
a groan.

(58) Those, he says, who introduce these particles
pointlessly are like actors who employ a word here or
a word there without meaning, as, for example, if one
were to say:

'This country is Calydon in the land of Pelops
                    (Ah me!),
And its fertile plains are across the straits
                    (Alas!)'.

As here the words 'ah me!' and 'alas' are dragged in
pointlessly, a similar effect is produced by an indiscriminate use of particles.

(59) Well, then, the particles introduce a stately effect
into the composition, as has been remarked, but the
figures of speech are themselves also a form of composition. To say the same words twice, whether by

repetition or by echoing or by paraphrasing, seems to be merely a matter of arrangement or composition. We must arrange suitable words for each character. For example, to the stately style, which is our present subject, we must assign the following.

(60) First of all, 'anthypallage', as in Homer: 'Now the two rocks—one indeed reaches the broad heaven'. Thus expressed, it is far more stately, with the case attracted, than if he had said: 'Of the two rocks, one indeed reaches the broad heaven'. That is the normal construction. Everything normal is unimpressive, and therefore fails to attract admiration.

(61) Nireus was unimportant and his following still more so, for it consisted of three ships and a few men. Yet Homer magnified him and multiplied his following by using a twofold figure of speech, combined from 'repetition' and 'disjunction'. He says: 'Nireus brought three ships, Nireus the son of Aglaïa, Nireus who was the fairest of men'. The repetition of language leading to the same name Nireus and the disjunction of phrases, suggest a large number of followers, although his forces consist only of two or three ships.

(62) Though the name of Nireus is barely mentioned once in the poem, we remember him as well as we remember Achilles and Odysseus, although they are referred to in almost every line. The reason for this is the power of the figure of language. If he had said: 'Nireus the son of Aglaïa brought three ships from Syme', he would appear to have passed over Nireus in silence. As in feasts, a few dishes arranged in a certain way seem many, in language the same result is seen.

(63) Often the opposite device to disjunction, namely, 'continuation', produces an impressive effect. For example: 'The expedition was joined by Greeks and Carians and Lycians and Pamphylians and Phrygians'.

The repetition of the same conjunction suggests an unlimited force.

(64) The expression 'arched, foam-crested' by reason of the omission of the conjunction 'and' causes a greater increase of dignity than if Homer had said, 'arched and foam-crested'.

(65) Dignity in composition is obtained by a variation of case, as in Thucydides: 'And he was the first to step on the gangway and he fainted away. Having fallen in the ship's bows, etc.' This gives a much greater dignity of style than if he had adhered to the same case and said: 'He fell on the ship's bows and lost his shield'.

(66) Tautology also produces stateliness, as in Herodotus: 'In some places in the Caucasus huge serpents were found—huge and many'. The repetition of the word 'huge' lends majesty to the style.

(67) The figures used should not be numerous. This shows lack of taste and an unevenness of style. However, the early writers employed many figures in their compositions, and yet were more natural than those who avoid them altogether, because they introduce them in an artistic way.

(68) With regard to hiatus of vowels, opinions differ. Isocrates and his pupils avoided it. Other writers introduce hiatus on all occasions and indiscriminately. It is a mistake to produce a noisy sentence, by a careless and indiscriminate collision of vowels—such action suggests a jerky and disjointed style—nor is it right completely to avoid a sequence of vowels. Perhaps the composition will thus be smoother, but it will be lacking in taste, and altogether dull, when deprived of the distinct musical quality which is produced by hiatus.

(69) We must consider first that constant usage brings vowels together in words, although it aims, above all,

at a musical effect, as in *Αἰακός* and *χίων*. Many words
are actually composed of vowels alone, as *Αἰαίη* and
Εὔιος; and yet these are no more unpleasing than any
others, but perhaps are even more melodious.

(70) Poetical words such as *ἠέλιος*, where the
division and the hiatus are intentional, and *ὀρέων*, are
more musical than *ἥλιος* and *ὁρῶν*. The division and
hiatus produce an effect of singing. Many other
expressions when united by elision are unmelodious,
but when divided by a hiatus are more melodious—as,
for example, *πάντα μὲν τὰ νέα καὶ καλά ἐστιν*. But if
you elide the vowel and say *καλᾶστιν*, the effect is less
melodious and more commonplace.

(71) In Egypt the priests sing hymns to the gods by
employing the seven vowels and uttering them in succession; the sound of these letters produces a musical
effect on the hearer which serves instead of flute and lyre.
To remove the hiatus would be to remove entirely the
melody and harmony of the language. But it is not
the right time now, perhaps, to enlarge on this theme.

(72) In the stately style an effective hiatus can be
produced by a conjunction of long vowels, as *λᾶαν ἄνω
ὤθεσκε* ('he heaved the rock upwards'). The line is
lengthened by the hiatus, and suggests the mighty
heaving of the stone. The same applies to the expression of Thucydides, *μὴ ἤπειρος εἶναι* ('so as not to
be joined to the mainland'). Diphthongs, also, may be
united to diphthongs: *ταύτην κατῴκησαν μὲν Κερκυραῖοι,
οἰκιστὴς δὲ ἐγένετο* . . . ('The Corcyraeans colonized it
—but its founder was . . .').

(73) The conjunction, then, of the same long vowels
and of the same diphthongs provides a stately effect.
But the conjunction of different vowels also produces
not only stateliness, but variety, through a multi-
plicity of sound; for example, *ἠώς*. Again, in the word

οἴην there is not only a difference of letters, but also of breathings, one being rough and the other smooth, so that there are many contrasts.

(74) In songs, also, trills are formed from one and the same long vowel, as though songs were piled upon songs. Therefore, the conjunction of similar sounds will form a small part of a song, or a trill. So much, then, for hiatus and the way in which it can contribute to stateliness of style.

(75) Stateliness is also derived from the subject-matter, should the theme be some eminent and famous land or sea battle, or deal with heaven or earth. He who hears some dignified theme is at once deceived into thinking that the narrator is using dignified language. But we shall not take into account the subject of the narrative so much as its character. It is possible, by describing eminent themes in an unimpressive way, to rob the subject of its dignity. Wherefore they say that certain powerful writers, like Theopompus, describe powerful subjects in a feeble manner.

(76) The painter Nicias was wont to say that the chief feature of the painter's art was to choose some impressive subject for his picture, and not fritter away his art on minute objects like little birds or flowers. He should choose cavalry or naval battles, in which he could show horses in all their movements—some galloping, some rearing, some sinking to the ground; and many riders shooting and many falling to the ground. He was of the opinion that the very choice of subject was a feature of the painter's art, just as the selection of legends is a feature of the poet's art. Nor is this surprising if in literature also stateliness is derived from a choice of stately themes.

(77) But in this style, the diction must be outstanding and uncommon and distinctive. Thus it will

acquire dignity; but the usual and familiar diction, though always clear, excites contempt.

(78) In the first place, then, metaphors must be introduced. These impart a charm and dignity to the composition. They should not, however, be too numerous; in that case we shall find ourselves writing dithyrambic poetry and not prose. Nor should they be far fetched, but derived from similar ideas close at hand. For example, there is a resemblance between a general, a pilot, and a chariot-driver. These are all rulers. It will, then, be quite safe to describe the general as 'the city's pilot', and conversely to describe the pilot as 'the ship's ruler'.

(79) However, not all metaphors are interchangeable, like those just mentioned. The poet was justified in calling the mountain-slope 'Ida's foot', but he would not be allowed to describe a man's foot as his 'mountain-slope'.

(80) When the metaphor seems dangerous, let it be changed into a simile. This will be safer. A simile is an extended metaphor. For example, you may take the metaphor, 'The poet Python, pouring down on you in a flood', and amplify it by saying 'pouring down on you *like* a flood'. So the figure has been converted into a simile, and it is safer. The former version is a metaphor and more dangerous. For this reason Plato seems to incur a certain amount of risk in his preference for metaphors to similes. Xenophon, however, prefers similes.

(81) In Aristotle's opinion, the best form of metaphor is the so-called 'active' metaphor, when inanimate objects are introduced as active, and endowed with life, as, for example, the passage about the shaft: 'The keen arrow leapt forth among the crowd on eager wings', and the passage, 'arched, foam-crested'. All such

expressions, as 'foam-crested' and 'on eager wings', suggest living activities.

(82) Some ideas, however, are described in metaphors with greater clearness and exactness than if exact language had been used—as the phrase 'the battle shivered'. No one, by paraphrasing this into exact language, could give a truer or clearer impression. The clash of spears, and the subsequent gentle and continuous murmur, is described as the battle shivering. At the same time the poet has, so to speak, utilized the active metaphor, mentioned above, when he described the battle as shivering like a living creature.

(83) We must, however, remember that some metaphors conduce to paltriness rather than to dignity, although the metaphor is employed to add weight, as in the line:

'All around, the great sky sounded a trumpet peal'.

The poet should not have compared the sound of the sky to the sound of a trumpet, unless you defend him by saying that the great sky resounded as if the whole sky was one great trumpet.

(84) Let us consider another kind of metaphor which conduces rather to paltriness than dignity. In our metaphors we must compare small objects to greater ones and not the opposite. Xenophon says, for example: 'When a portion of the company surged out, on the march'. He compared a deviation from the ranks to a surging sea, and so applied his metaphor. If, on the contrary, he had spoken of the sea as 'deviating from its ranks', the metaphor would be, perhaps, inappropriate; it would certainly be utterly paltry.

(85) Some writers secure their metaphors by the addition of epithets, when they seem dangerous; Theognis, for example, applies the expression, 'a chordless lyre', to a bow when he describes someone shooting.

The term 'lyre' seemed a dangerous metaphor to describe a bow, and so it was rendered secure by the epithet 'chordless'.

(86) Custom, which teaches us all else, is especially a teacher of metaphors. It applies metaphors almost universally, and yet it escapes notice by using safe metaphors. It speaks of a 'silvery' voice and a 'keen' man, and a 'rough' nature, and a 'lengthy' orator, and so forth. These metaphors are applied with such good taste that they seem to be literally true.

(87) I lay down the criterion for the use of metaphors in composition, viz. 'art, or nature, established by custom'. Custom describes some ideas so well by metaphor, that we no longer need literal words; the metaphor remains, usurping the place of the original word—as, for example, 'the eye of the vine' and other similar expressions.

(88) The parts of the body are called σφόνδυλος (spine), κλείς (collar-bone), and κτένες (fingers). These are not metaphors, but similes, because they resemble, respectively, a spindle, a key, and a comb.

(89) When we convert a metaphor into a simile, in the manner described, we must aim at conciseness and at adding nothing but the word 'like', otherwise it would not be a simile, but a poetical comparison. Xenophon, for example, says: 'Like a noble dog which bounds recklessly upon a boar', or 'Like a horse, free from control, which gallops and prances over the plain'. These have no longer any resemblance to similes, but rather to poetical comparisons.

(90) We must not lightly introduce these comparisons into prose, nor without great care. So much, then, for our sketch of the metaphor.

(91) We must also introduce compound words, but must not coin them after the fashion of dithyrambic

poets, such as, 'God-portented wanderings', or 'the fire-speared host of the stars'. We must use words which resemble those composed by established custom. To give a general rule, I make custom the criterion of all word-coining. This gives us 'law-makers' and 'master-builders', and is a sure guide in framing many other such words.

(92) However, the compound word will possess a distinction and dignity from its formation, and at the same time a kind of conciseness. A word will be substituted for the whole phrase, as if, for example, you speak of 'food-convoy' instead of the convoy of food. It is much better thus. Perhaps also, conversely, dignity may be attained by resolving the word into a phrase, as if you substitute 'the convoy of food' for 'food-convoy'.

(93) A word is substituted for a phrase when, for example, Xenophon says that it was impossible to catch a wild ass unless the horses stood at intervals and hunted it by relays. The word used for 'by relays' suggests that those behind were pursuing, while the others rode in front to meet them, so that the ass was caught between the two parties. We must, however, be careful to avoid making many compound words. This practice travels beyond the scope of prose composition.

(94) We define words which are coined, as those which are spoken in imitation of some emotion or action, as, for example, 'hiss' or 'lapping'.

(95) These create an impression of stateliness because they resemble the sound, and especially by their novel character.

The writer does not use existing words, but words which are coming into existence while he writes. At the same time, the creation of a new word, as though it were already familiar, seems a sign of poetic inspiration.

As a word-maker the poet seems to resemble those who first gave names to objects.

(96) We must aim first at clearness and familiarity in the coining of words; next at similarity with words already existing, so that we may not seem to introduce Phrygian or Scythian terms into a Greek vocabulary.

(97) We must either coin words for objects that have no names, like the man who described kettledrums and all other effeminate instruments as κιναιδίαι, and, like Aristotle, who invented the term 'elephant-driver', or when a writer invents words on the analogy of existing words, like the man who described someone sculling a boat as a 'sculler', or Aristotle, who described a man who was alone as a 'solitary' (αὐτίτης).

(98) Xenophon says that the army 'bravoed', indicating by the word the cry 'bravo', which the army kept on raising. However, the practice of coining words is dangerous, as I said, even for the poets themselves. The compound word may be described as a kind of coined word. Everything which is compounded is undoubtedly formed from some existing matter.

(99) Allegory is also an example of sublime language; this particularly applies to threats, as when Dionysius said that 'the cicalas shall sing to them from the ground'.

(100) If he had spoken plainly and said that he was about to ravage Locris, he would have appeared more irritable and less impressive. As it was he used the allegory to veil his language. Anything spoken in a riddle is more alarming, and different people interpret it in different ways. What is clear and evident is apt to excite contempt, just like men who have stripped themselves naked.

(101) For this reason the mysteries are veiled in allegories in order to inspire awe and horror, and to

suggest darkness and night. In fact, the allegory suggests darkness and night.

(102) But in this figure, too, we must beware of excess, in order that our language may not become a riddle, as in the description of the doctor's cupping-glass: 'I saw a man welding with fire brass upon a man'. The Lacedemonians often used allegorical language to inspire fear, like the message to Philip, 'Dionysius in Corinth', and many other similar sayings.

(103) Conciseness in some cases has a stately effect, and above all, aposiopesis. Some ideas seem more impressive when not uttered but merely hinted at. In some cases, on the other hand, it has a feeble effect. Repetition is impressive, as when Xenophon said: 'The chariots were borne on their way, some through the very ranks of their friends, and some through the very ranks of their enemies'. This is much more effective than if he had said, 'through the ranks both of their friends and of their enemies'.

(104) Often an indirect expression is more effective than a straightforward sentence. For example: 'Their idea was that of driving into the ranks of the Greeks and cutting their way through', instead of saying, 'They intended to drive and cut their way'.

(105) Assurance and apparent harshness of sound is also helpful. Harshness often adds dignity, as in the line: 'Ajax the mighty always against Hector'. The conjunction of the two words $A\ddot{\iota}\alpha\varsigma$ and $\alpha\iota\acute{\epsilon}\nu$ does much more to indicate the greatness of Ajax than does his shield of seven hides.

(106) The so-called 'epiphonema' can be defined as 'diction that embellishes'. It is the most dignified figure in compositions. Diction sometimes helps the idea, and sometimes embellishes it. In the following instances it helps it: 'Even like the hyacinth which on

the mountains shepherds tread underfoot'. The expression which follows, adds embellishment: 'And on the ground the purple flower lies'. In this there is a clear addition to the preceding lines of grace and beauty.

(107) Homer's poetry, too, is full of these figures; for example: 'Out of the smoke have I laid them by, since they are no longer like those which Odysseus left behind him of old, when he went to Troy. Moreover, some God hath put into my heart this other and greater care, lest perchance when ye are heated with wine, ye set a quarrel between you and wound one the other'. Then he adds the epiphonema: 'For iron of itself draws a man thereto'.

(108) To speak generally, the epiphonema is like the embellishments of wealthy men, cornices, triglyphs, and broad purple bands. It is, as it were, itself a sign of wealth in language.

(109) The enthymeme, too, might seem to be a kind of epiphonema, but really it is not. It is introduced, not to add grace, but to convince; it is, however, appended like an epiphonema.

(110) Similarly, a proverb resembles an epiphonema, which is added to a previous statement, but it is not the same figure. In fact, it often comes first, but it may take the last place like an epiphonema.

(111) The line: 'Fool that he was; he was not destined to escape the evil fates', is not an epiphonema either. It is not added at the end, nor does it add grace, nor does it resemble an epiphonema in any respect, but rather an address or a taunt.

(112) Poetical language in prose lends sublimity, as is clear even to a blind man. However, some introduce a bold imitation of the poets; or rather they do not imitate them, but borrow from them, like Herodotus.

(113) Thucydides, however, even if he transfers a

phrase from a poet, treats it in an individual way and makes what he has borrowed his own. For example, the poet, in speaking of Crete, said: 'There is a land called Crete in the midst of the wine-dark sea, a fair land and a rich and sea-begirt'. He used the word 'sea-begirt' in reference to its size. Thucydides, however, thinks it a fine ideal for the Sicilian Greeks to live in harmony, since they inhabit one land and that 'sea-begirt'. Although he uses exactly the same terms, 'land' for 'island' and 'sea-begirt', nevertheless his language seems different, because he did not apply these words to the size of the island, but to its unity. This, then, is enough on the stately style.

(114) As there are base qualities which correspond to noble qualities—for example, recklessness corresponds to courage and shame to awe—so the forms of style have certain perverted forms which correspond to them. First I will speak of a style which borders on the stately. Its name is 'frigid', and Theophrastus defines it thus: 'A frigid style is that which transcends the appropriate language', as, for example: 'An unbased cup is not entabled'; by which the writer means that 'a cup without a base is not set upon the table'. The triviality of the object does not admit of so extravagant a style.

(115) Frigidity, like stateliness, rests on three qualities. One of these is the idea, as in describing the Cyclops throwing a stone at the ship of Odysseus, a certain writer said that while the stone was hurtling through the air, there were goats grazing on it. The frigidity arises from the exaggeration and the impossibility of the idea.

(116) Aristotle says that frigidity arises in diction from four causes, namely [in the use of rare words, and in the misuse of epithets] as when Alcidamus speaks of 'damp sweat'; or in the use of compound words, when

the combination of expressions is formed in a dithyrambic way, as when someone coined the word 'lonely-
wandering', or any other such extravagant phrase.
Frigidity is also found in metaphors, as 'His condition
was trembling and pallid'. These, then, are the four
errors of diction which cause frigidity.

(117) Composition is frigid when it has a bad rhythm
or none, and when it consists wholly of long syllables,
like the following: ἥκων ἡμῶν εἰς τὴν χώραν, πάσης ἡμῶν
ὀρθῆς οὔσης. The passage is lacking in prose-value and
in security through its succession of long syllables.

(118) Frigidity also results from introducing continuous
metrical passages, as some writers do, when their constant succession brings them to notice. Poetry out of
place is just as frigid as verse which does not scan.

(119) To speak generally, frigidity is somewhat akin
to boastfulness. The braggart claims qualities as his
own which do not belong to him, and the writer who uses
exaggerated language over trifles is like one who boasts
about trifles. The proverbial 'embossed pestle' suggests the literary style which expresses trivial matters
in exaggerated terms.

(120) Still, there are those who claim that it is right
to use a grand style for small themes, and claim that this
is a sign of surpassing power. I, for my part, agree
with the orator Polycrates who eulogized [Thersites]
as he might have done Agamemnon by the use of antithesis, metaphor, and all the adjuncts of eulogy. He
was writing in jest and not in earnest; the very exaggeration of style is a form of jest. Let him have his jest,
I say, but we must always preserve propriety; by this
I mean that style must be appropriate to its subject—
a modest style to a modest subject, and a grand style
to a grand subject.

(121) Xenophon is an example when he speaks of

the lovely little river Teleboas: 'This river was not
great, but was beautiful'. By the conciseness of his
sentence and by the position of the conjunction δέ he
almost brought its smallness before our eyes. Another
writer, when writing of a river similar to the Teleboas,
said: 'It finds its source in the hills of Laurium and discharges into the sea', as though he were describing the
cataracts of the Nile or the estuary of the Danube.
All such passages are described as frigid.

(122) Small subjects are magnified in another way,
not by inappropriate language, but sometimes from sheer
necessity; for example, when we wish to extol a general
who has had some trifling success, as though he had
performed some brilliant achievement, or when we
justify the ephor at Sparta who scourged a man for
playing ball in an elegant way instead of the local way.
Though the offence sounds but trifling, we invest it with
a tragic importance. We say that those who pass
over small misdeeds are opening the door to graver
crimes, and that the right principle is to inflict severe
punishment on little misdemeanours, and not wait for
graver ones. We shall add the proverb, 'The beginning
is half the deed', or say that this is suitable to a small
crime, and in fact, that no crime is small.

(123) In this way it may be regarded as lawful to
magnify some trifling success, but not in an unbecoming
manner. As what is great can often be usefully belittled,
so some small achievement can be extolled.

(124) Hyperbole is the most frigid of all figures of
speech. It takes three forms. It may be expressed
in the form of a comparison, as in the phrase 'swift as
the winds in running', it may claim superiority, as
'whiter than the snow', or it may claim the impossible,
as 'She smote the sky with her head'.

(125) Every hyperbole is impossible. Nothing could

be whiter than snow, and nothing could run as fast as the winds. This third hyperbole, however, is specially described as 'impossible'. Therefore, every hyperbole seems to be an example of frigidity because it seems impossible.

(126) The reason why comic poets make a frequent use of this figure, is that they introduce laughter from an impossible situation. For example, a comic poet, in describing the voracity of the Persians, said, in exaggerated terms: 'They voided whole plains', and 'they carried oxen in their jaws'.

(127) To the same class of language belongs the phrase 'balder than a cloudless sky', and 'healthier than a pumpkin'. The expression of Sappho, 'more golden than gold', is hyperbolical and impossible, but it possesses charm by its very impossibility and is not frigid. In fact, the most admirable quality of the divine Sappho is that she makes use of language which is naturally dangerous and intractable, and produces an effect of charm. This, then, will suffice for frigidity and hyperbole. I will now proceed to speak of the polished style.

III

(128) The polished style possesses grace and brightness. Some ornaments of language, those of the poets, are somewhat stately and impressive; others are more commonplace and amusing, resembling jests, like those of Aristotle, Sophron, and Lysias. The following witticisms: 'It would be easier to count her teeth than her fingers'—referring to an old woman; and 'For every blow he deserved, he received instead a shilling'— these and such as these are practically gibes, and differ little from comedy.

(129) But the passages from Homer: 'And the Nymphs too sport at her side, and Leto rejoices in her heart', and 'Easy to distinguish is she; and yet all of them are fair'—these passages are ornaments which are described as impressive and stately.

(130) Homer uses them sometimes to make a passage telling and effective. When he is playful he is the more awe-inspiring; and he seems to have been the first to invent graces of languages that inspire awe. For example, in dealing with that very repulsive person the Cyclops, he says: 'Noman I will eat last; the rest I will eat first'. This is the guest-present of the Cyclops. By no other detail does he depict him in such a horrible light, neither when he devours the two companions, nor by his cave-door, nor by his club, as he does by this witticism.

(131) Xenophon also uses a similar device, and he derives startling effects from ornaments of style; for example, in the passage about the armed dancing-girl. When one of his characters was asked by the Paphlagonian whether women also shared in their warfare, he replied: 'Yes; for they actually put the great king to flight'. The startling effect produced by this expression is twofold. First, they were not accompanied by mere women, but by Amazons. The second was at the expense of the great king, who was so feeble as to be routed by women.

(132) The ornaments of style, then, have such varieties and such characteristics. Sometimes they are derived from the subject-matter; for example, the gardens of the Nymphs, wedding lays, love stories—in fact, the whole of Sappho's poetry. Such themes, even on the lips of a Hipponax, possess a charm, and the subject itself has a brightness of its own. No one could sing a wedding-lay when overcome with anger; no trick of

style could transform Love into a Fury or a Giant, or convert laughter into tears.

(133) There is, then, a kind of ornament in the subject-matter; sometimes the style, too, adds further grace, as, for example: 'Even as when the daughter of Pandareus, the brown-bright nightingale, sings sweet in the first season of the spring'. In this passage we have the charming little bird, the nightingale, and the charming season of spring. But the idea has been embellished greatly by the style, and acquires an additional charm by the application of the words 'brown-bright' and 'daughter of Pandareus', to a bird. These additions belong to the poet.

(134) Often the subject-matter is naturally unattractive and even repulsive, but a touch of brightness is added by the writer. This invention, it seems, was due first to Xenophon. He took the unattractive and repulsive person of Aglaitadas, the Persian, and derived from him an amusing jest. 'It is easier', he said, 'to extract fire than laughter from you.'

(135) This is the most striking ornament, and it depends entirely on the writer. The subject-matter was naturally repulsive and opposed to charm, namely Aglaitadas. But he shows that humour can be extracted from even such material as this; that one can, so to speak, be cooled by heat and warmed by cold.

(136) Now that we have pointed out the different kinds of ornaments of style, what they are, and where they are found, it remains to state the sources from which they are derived. They consist, as we have seen, partly in diction, and partly in subject-matter. We will now show the sources of each, and will begin with diction.

(137) At once we find that the first ornament is due to conciseness, when the same theme treated at length

lacks grace. A rapid touch lends charm, as in Xenophon: 'This fellow really has no connection with Hellas, for I saw him with both his ears pierced, like a Lydian. And so it was'. The closing words: 'And so it was', impart charm from their conciseness. If the passage had been expanded thus, 'What he said was true. It was clear that his ears had been pierced', it would have been a bald narrative and no ornament of style.

(138) Often, also, two ideas are expressed in one to produce a graceful effect, as, for example, in reference to the sleeping Amazon, a writer said: 'Her bow lay strung, and her quiver full, her shield beneath her head. Their girdles they loose not'. Herein is expressed both the custom about the girdle, and the fact that she did not loose her girdle. Two facts are conveyed in one expression. This conciseness gives a certain amount of polish.

(139) A second source comes from the order. The same words when placed first or in the middle lack charm, but at the end they are graceful. For example, Xenophon says of Cyrus: 'He presents him with gifts, a horse, a robe, a necklet, and a promise that his land shall be no more ravaged'. In this list, the last is the one that creates its charm, the promise that his land shall be no more ravaged. The gift is strange and unique. The position of the clause constitutes the charm. If it had been placed first, it would have possessed less charm—if, for example, he had said: 'He presents him with gifts, a promise that his land shall be no more ravaged, and a horse, a robe, and a necklet'. As it is, he begins with the usual gifts, and adds last the strange and unusual gift, and it is from these facts that the charm is derived.

(140) The ornaments derived from figures of speech are clear and seen most frequently in Sappho; an

instance of this is 'redoubling'. A bride somewhere is addressing her maidenhood, and says: 'Maidenhood, Maidenhood, whither dost thou go and desert me?' And the Maidenhood uses the same figure in her reply: 'No more will I come to thee; no more will I come'. A greater charm is conveyed than if the words had been spoken once and the figure had not been used. And yet the repetition seems to have been invented to express power. But Sappho uses the most powerful figures to impart grace.

(141) Sometimes also she imparts grace by 'anaphora', as in the passage on the evening star: 'Evening star, thou bringest all things; thou bringest the sheep, thou bringest the goat, thou bringest the child to his mother'. Here, too, the grace is derived from the word 'bringest', which is repeated with the same application.

(142) Many other instances of graceful sentences could be quoted. They are derived from diction or from metaphor, as in the passage about the cicala: 'From beneath its wings it pours forth a clear strain, to whatever fiery height it soars and warbles'.

(143) They are derived also from compound words of the dithyrambic style:

> 'Pluto, lord of black-pinioned creatures,
> Do this strange deed, before their wings'.

These are playful expressions, suitable to comedy and satyric drama.

(144) Another source of ornament is derived from unusual words, as when Aristotle says: 'The more lonesome I am, the more I become a myth-lover'. Coined words are another source; Aristotle says in the same passage: 'The more selfful and lonesome I am, the more I become a lover of fables'. The word 'lonesome' is of a rather

unusual nature; and the word 'selfful' is coined from 'self.'

(145) Many words derive their charm from being applied to a particular thing. For example: 'This bird is a flatterer and a knave'. Here the charm is due to chiding the bird as if it were a man, and the fact that unusual terms were applied to the bird. Such ornaments of style are due simply to the diction.

(146) Another source of literary polish comes from the use of comparison; as, for example, when Sappho is speaking of a leading man, and says: 'He was distinguished like the Lesbian bard amid aliens'. Here, grace rather than stateliness is derived from the comparison. She might have said, 'distinguished like the morn as compared with the stars', or 'as the sun excels in brilliance', or any other more poetical expressions.

(147) Sophron, too, uses the same device when he says: 'Behold, all the leaves and twigs wherewith the children are pelting the man; 'tis, my dear, even as they say the Trojans pelted Ajax with mud'. Here the comparison possesses grace, and playfully suggests that the Trojans were children.

(148) Sappho derives a charm of her own from recantation, when she says something and recants and, as it were, repents. For example: 'Ye builders, raise the hall on high. A bridegroom is entering like unto Ares—far taller than a man of high stature'. She checks herself, as it were, as she had used an impossible exaggeration. No man is as tall as Ares.

(149) Similar is the passage in the story of Telemachus: 'Two hounds were chained before the portal. I would tell you even the names of the hounds. But what, pray, would these names mean?' The writer here cleverly changed his mind and suppressed the names.

(150) Charm is derived from quoting another writer, as when Aristophanes twits Zeus for not striking the

wicked with thunder, and says: 'His own temple he strikes, and "Sunium the headland of Athens"'! It seems that it is no longer Zeus who is exposed to ridicule, but Homer and the line of Homer. By this device the charm is heightened.

(151) Some allegories have also a touch of the commonplace, as, for example: 'Delphians, your bitch is bearing a child'. Also Sophron's reference to the aged men: 'Here I too, among you, whose hair is white like mine, wait to put out to sea till the voyage be fair; yea since for such as us the anchors are already weighed'. He makes other similar allegories about women, on the matter of fish: 'Razor-fish and shell-fish whose flavour is sweet, delicacies dear to widows'. Such writings savour of low comedy and are in bad taste.

(152) Charm comes also from the unexpected—like the saying of the Cyclops, 'Noman will I eat last'. Such a guest-gift was wholly unexpected, both by Odysseus and by the reader. Aristophanes, also, in reference to Socrates, says: 'He melted the wax and then took a compass, and from the wrestling-school he stole a coat'.

(153) Here the charm is derived from two sources. Not only was the closing idea quite unexpected, but it had no connection in sense with what preceded. Such a lack of sequence bears the name 'griphos', and an illustration is seen in Boulias, the prater in the play of Sophron. All his remarks are wholly unconnected. Menander's prologue to his play *Messenia* gives another instance.

(154) Often a similarity of members adds polish, as in the saying of Aristotle: 'I came from Athens to Stageira, because of the great king; and from Stageira to Athens, because of the great storm'. By closing both the members on the same word he adds a polish

to his style. If you remove the word 'great' from each member, you will also remove the polish.

(155) Sometimes veiled reproaches have an appearance of grace; for example, in Xenophon, Heracleides, who was in company with Seuthes, went up to his fellow-guests and persuaded them each to offer to Seuthes whatever gift he had. This passage shows a kind of grace, and veiled reproaches as well.

(156) I have described the polish which is connected with the style, and also the sources whence it is derived. Subject-matter also creates polish—for example, by the use of proverbs. A proverb possesses a natural charm. Sophron speaks of 'Epioles who strangled his father'. Elsewhere he says: 'He painted the lion from the claw. He polished the ladle. He divided the cummin'.[1] He uses two or three proverbs in succession, that his writings may overflow with charm. In fact, it is almost possible to make a complete collection of all proverbs from his dramas.

(157) The timely introduction of a fable adds grace. It may be a well-known fable, as when Aristotle says of the eagle: 'It dies of hunger because its beak grows bent. It suffers such a fate because once when human it injured a guest'. Here he uses a well-established and familiar fable.

(158) We also invent many appropriate fables which have a bearing on our subject. A certain writer quotes the legend: 'The cat pines and grows with the waning and waxing of the moon'. He then adds the following, from his own invention: 'Hence arises the fable that the moon gave birth to the cat'. There will not only be found charm in the art of invention; but the fable itself suggests a pleasing idea that a cat is the moon's child.

[1] Proverbial expression implying: (a) large conclusions from slender premises, (b) wasted labour, (c) niggardliness.

(159) Charm often arises from a groundless fear, as when someone is filled with needless terror at a strap, mistaking it for a serpent, or a baking-pan, which he imagines to be a chasm in the ground. Such situations belong rather to comedy.

(160) Similes, too, possess charm, as when you compare the cock to a Persian, because he has an upright crest, or to the great king, because he is clad in purple, or because we leap up at the note of the cock, as we would leap in alarm at the voice of the king.

(161) Exaggeration possesses a charm, especially in comedies. Every exaggeration expresses an impossibility, as when Aristophanes, describing the voracity of the Persians, says: 'They baked oxen in bread-pans, instead of loaves'. Another refers to the Thracians, and says: 'Their king Medoces carried a whole ox in his jaws'.

(162) The following expressions belong to the same class: 'healthier than a pumpkin', and 'balder than the blue sky', and the words of Sappho, 'more melodious than a shepherd's pipe, more golden than gold'. Ornaments of style like these are derived from exaggeration.

(163) The ridiculous differs from the graceful, first in its subject-matter. Gardens of nymphs, loves, are the material that supplies grace, but they do not provoke mirth. They will differ as much as Thersites and Eros.

(164) They differ also in the very language. Graceful language is accompanied by ornament, and is expressed by the medium of beautiful words, which do most to add charm; for example: 'The myriad-garlanded earth is broidered like a robe', and the 'brown-bright nightingale'. The ridiculous is composed of ordinary commonplace language, like the sentence: 'The more selfful and lonesome I am, the more I become a lover of fables'.

(165) Again, the ridiculous loses its character when adorned by style and becomes impressive instead. However, the graces of style must be used with moderation. To embellish the ridiculous is like beautifying an ape.

(166) Therefore, when Sappho sings of beauty she chooses beautiful and sweet words—she does the same when she sings of loves and of spring and of kingfishers. Every lovely word is woven into the fabric of her poetry; some words too she created herself.

(167) Very different is the way in which she jeers at the uncouth bridegroom and the porter at the wedding. She uses everyday language, and the diction of prose rather than of poetry, so that these poems are more suitable to recite than to sing. They will not accommodate themselves to the chorus or the lyre, unless you could find a conversational chorus.

(168) They differ most in their purpose. The graceful writer and the provoker of mirth have wholly different aims. The one wishes to gladden, and the other to be laughed at. They differ also in their results, which are in the latter case, laughter, and in the former, praise.

(169) They differ also in province. It is true that the arts of ridicule and charm are found combined in the satyric drama and in comedy. Tragedy, however, often calls in the aid of grace, but mirth is repugnant to tragedy. No one could imagine tragedy indulging in jest. He who does so will be a writer of satyric drama and not tragedy.

(170) Even sensible men will sometimes use jests in season, for example, at feasts and drinking-parties, and in reprimanding those given to luxurious living. The phrase, 'far-shining meal-bag' may be used of the poetry of Crates; or you might read 'A eulogy of

lentils' at a gathering of prodigals. This method is
rather that of the Cynics. Such jests as these assume
the role of maxims and proverbs.

(171) An indication of character is seen in a man's
jests—if they be playful or scurrilous. Someone once
stopped the spilling of wine with a remark about
'Peleus instead of Oineus' (i.e. mud instead of wine).
However, a laboured punning on names indicates an
ill-bred and undisciplined nature.

(172) In nicknames a kind of comparison is suggested.
To play on names requires a ready wit. Men will use
the following kind of comparisons: 'Egyptian clematis'
for a tall, dark man; 'a marine sheep' for a fool on a
voyage. They may indulge in such expressions as these;
but for the most part, we had better shun such gibes
as we would vulgar abuse.

(173) So-called 'beautiful words' create a graceful
style. Theophrastus defined them thus: 'A word is
beautiful if it suggests some agreeable sound or sight,
or inspires some noble thought'.

(174) Such words as these suggest agreeable sights:
'rose-tinted', 'flower-laden hue'. Sights which bring
pleasure to the eye, are beautiful also to the ear. The
following are agreeable in sound: 'Callistratos; Annoön'.
The double 'l' and the double 'n' have an attractive
sound.

(175) To speak generally, it is for the sake of euphony
that the Attic writers add an 'n' to the accusatives of
Demosthenes and Socrates. There are words which
suggest some ennobling thought, such as 'the ancients',
which has a finer ring than 'the men of old'. The word
implies a higher esteem.

(176) Musicians speak of a smooth word, a rough
word, a compact word, and a heavy word. A smooth
word is composed either wholly or principally of vowels,

for example, *Αἴας*. An example of a rough word is
βέβρωκεν. The very roughness is due to the fact that
the sound imitates the action. A compact word is a
blend of the two, and in it vowels and consonants are
equally combined.

(177) Weight consists of three qualities: breadth,
length, and formation. βροντά, for example, is substituted for βροντή. The first syllable gives it roughness; the second gives it length, because of the long
vowel, and breadth because of the Doric vowel. The
Dorians always broaden their vowels, and therefore no
one wrote comedies in Dorian dialect, but only in keen
Attic. The Attic dialect has something concise and
popular and suitable to such pleasantries.

(178) This digression must be forgiven. Of the words
mentioned we may use only those which are smooth as
possessing polish.

(179) Polish is derived also from the composition.
It is not easy to describe how this is attained. None of
the former writers have treated of polish in composition.
Still, I must try to describe it as best I can.

(180) No doubt a pleasant and graceful effect will be
produced if we adapt a metrical system wholly or par-
tially to our composition. This should not be done in
such a way that the actual metres may be apparent
when the sentences are joined; but if they were dis-
sected and analysed, then we ought to be able to detect
the existence of metre.

(181) If there be but a suggestion of metre, it will
produce the same pleasing effect. Imperceptibly the
charm of such a pleasant practice steals into our mind.
Such a system is used mostly by the Peripatetics and
by Plato and Xenophon and Herodotus; perhaps
also Demosthenes uses it in places, but Thucydides
never.

(182) An example can be quoted from Dichaearchus, who says: 'In Elia on Italian soil, an aged man advanced in years'. The close of each of the members has a metrical cadence, but the metre is disguised by the way in which the phrases are joined and linked; yet a very pleasing effect is produced.

(183) Plato often acquires polish by his very rhythm, which is somehow different, and has neither weight nor length. The former suits the plain and powerful style; the latter belongs to the stately style. His members produce a gliding effect; they are neither wholly metrical nor unmetrical, as, for example, in his description of music, opening with the words: 'A moment ago I was saying'.

(184) Again, 'In warbling and beneath the spell of music's charm he wholly spends his life'; and again, 'First if he had any spirited vein in his soul, like steel he tempers it'. Such a passage has polish and a clear element of music. Should you alter the order and say, 'he tempers it as if it were steel', or 'he spends the whole of his life', you rob the passage of its grace, which consists in the very rhythm. It certainly consists neither in the sentiment nor in the language.

(185) In speaking, too, of musical instruments, again he blends his words in a graceful fashion. He says in the context: 'The lyre is left to you in your state'. If you invert the order and say 'in your state it is left', you will be practically altering the rhythm. He adds: 'And further in the fields the shepherds would have some manner of pipe'. By extending and lengthening his sentence, he produces a very pleasing imitation of the note of the pipe. You will see this clearly if you invert the order of this passage also and then recite it.

(186) I have said enough about the appearance of polish, when due to the order of the words,

for the subject is difficult. I have spoken, too, of the features of the polished style, and shown on what it depends and whence it is derived. As there was a frigid style which corresponded to the stately style, so also there is a similar perversion corresponding to the polished style. I apply to this the popular name of 'affectation'. This, too, like the rest, falls into three headings.

(187) First it depends on the sense, as when a writer described the centaur as 'riding on his own back', and when Alexander was meditating on competing in the races at Olympia, someone said: 'Alexander, race along thy mother's name' (i.e. Olympias).

(188) Secondly, it may be found in the words, as 'the fragrant-hued rose was smiling'. The metaphor of 'smiling' is applied most unsuitably, and the compound word 'fragrant-hued' would not be used even in poetry by a writer of sound judgment. Again, a writer said: 'The pine was piping softly to the gentle breezes'. This will suffice, then, for diction.

(189) Thirdly, it is found in an anapaestic rhythm, which most nearly resembles broken and undignified metres, like those of Sotades, with their effeminate ring. The following are examples: 'Having dried it with heat, let it lie'; and 'As he brandishes ashes of Pelion upwards his shoulder above', instead of 'Brandishing the Pelion ash over his shoulder'. The line seems to be transformed, like those people in fable who are changed from men to women. So much, then, on the subject of affectation.

IV

(190) In treating of the plain style we might, perhaps, introduce certain commonplace themes which are well adapted to this style—for example, the passage in Lysias: 'I have a little two-storied cottage, in which the upper story exactly matches the lower'.

The style must be wholly normal and familiar. The more commonplace the theme, the more familiar is the style. Unfamiliar and far-fetched diction belong to the stately style.

(191) Compound words are out of place. These, too, belong to the opposite style; so are coined words, in fact all which produce stately language. Above all, the language must be clear. Clearness depends on a number of qualities.

(192) First it requires normal words, and secondly, a use of conjunctions. Asyndeton and loose connection is always lacking in clearness. It is uncertain where each member begins because of the loose connection. This is seen in Heracleitus. His loose style is the principal cause of his obscurity.

(193) Unconnected style is, perhaps, more suitable for oratory; it is also called theatrical, because loose sentences encourage acting. A literary style, on the other hand, is agreeable to read. This style is connected and secured by conjunctions. For this reason actors prefer Menander, because his style is often disjointed, while Philemon appeals to readers.

(194) A single example will serve to show that looseness of style suits the stage: 'I received thee, I bore thee, I nurse thee, my child'. The sentence thus disconnected will compel you to act the passage, whether you will or no, because of its broken character. If you

join the sentences and say, 'I received thee and I bore thee and I nurse thee', you will lose much feeling by the conjunctions. Any passage devoid of feeling is unsuited to the stage.

(195) There are also other dramatic factors. For example, in Euripides, Ion seizes the bow and threatens the swan which was bespattering the statues. Many movements are suggested to the actor by Ion dashing for the bow, and turning his face up to the sky while he reasons with the swan. In fact, the whole character of the scene is constructed to meet the actor's needs. However, we are not now discussing drama.

(196) Clear writing must avoid ambiguity; it should adopt a figure known as 'epanalepsis' or repetition. 'Epanalepsis' consists of repeating the same conjunction in the course of a long passage, for example: 'All the deeds that Philip did, and how he subdued Thrace and took the Chersonese and besieged Byzantium, and refused to restore Amphipolis—this I will pass over'. The repetition of the conjunction goes a long way to remind us of the opening, and recalls us back to the beginning of the paragraph.

(197) For the sake of lucidity we must often repeat ourselves. What conciseness gains by being attractive it loses by being obscure. As men running past us often pass unrecognized, so language, too, is not taken in if its movement is rapid.

(198) We must avoid also oblique cases. This, too, causes obscurity, as is shown by the style of Philistus, though it may be less diffuse. An example of the oblique style, which is on this account obscure, is seen in Xenophon: 'He was told that triremes were sailing from Ionia to Cilicia, with Tamos on board—the triremes, which belonged to the Lacedaemonians and to Cyrus himself'. This sentence could be expressed in straight-

forward language as follows: 'Many Lacedaemonian vessels were expected to arrive at Cilicia, and many Persian vessels also, which had been built by Cyrus for this very purpose. They were sailing from Ionia, and Tamos the Egyptian was the admiral in command of them'. Stated thus the passage is perhaps longer, but it is clearer.

(199) To speak generally, we must use the natural order of the words; for example: 'Epidamnus is a city on your right hand as you sail into the Ionian gulf'. First in the order comes the subject, secondly the predicate— that it is a city; the other facts then follow.

(200) The order might be reversed; for example: 'There is a city Ephyre'. We do not approve of this order for every occasion, nor do we reject the former, as we are simply putting forward the natural form of the order of words.

(201) In narrative passages we ought either to begin with the nominative, 'Epidamnus is a city', or with the accusative, 'It is said that the city Epidamnus'. All other cases will tend to obscurity, and will puzzle both the speaker and the hearer.

(202) We must try not to prolong our periods unduly, as in the following: 'The river Achelous, which flows from Mount Pindus passing by the town Stratos, discharges into the sea'. It would be better here to give a pause and a rest to the ear, and say: 'The Achelous flows from Mount Pindus, and discharges into the sea'. So expressed it is much clearer, like roads which have many sign-posts and many halting-places. Sign-posts are like guides. A monotonous road without sign-posts, however short it is, seems hard to follow.

(203) This, then, will suffice on the subject of clearness, though much more might be said. Clearness is the principal requisite in the plain style.

(204) In composition of this kind we must first avoid long members. Length is always a mark of stateliness, just as in metres the hexameter, because of its length, is called 'heroic' and is suitable to heroes; the New Comedy, on the other hand, adopts the shorter trimeter.

(205) We shall commonly use trimeter members and sometimes short clauses, as in Plato's opening: 'I went down yesterday to the Peiraeus with Glaucon'. This sentence contains a number of pauses and rests. Aeschines, too, says: 'We were sitting on the benches in the Lyceum, where the stewards arrange the contest'.

(206) The ends of the members should have a definite rest and basis, as in the examples quoted. Prolonged endings are marks of the stately style, as in Thucydides: 'The river Achelous, which flows from Mount Pindus, etc.'

(207) We must avoid also, in this style, the union of long vowels and of diphthongs. There is always something pompous in length. We must either join short vowels with short, as πάντα μὲν τὰ νέα καλά ἐστιν, or short with long, as ἠέλιος, or somehow or other express ourselves with short vowels. To speak generally, such a form of diction is apt to seem unimpressive and commonplace, and it is composed with this end in view.

(208) Pedantic figures must also be avoided. Anything that is conspicuous is unusual and unnatural. This style will be marked principally by lucidity and persuasiveness. We will speak, then, of lucidity and persuasiveness.

(209) We will deal first with lucidity. This quality is derived first from accuracy, and from not omitting or cutting out any idea. For example, take the simile in Homer which begins with the words, 'And as a man makes a conduit, etc.'. Its lucidity is due to the fact that every little incident is expressed and nothing is omitted.

(210) Take again the chariot-race in memory of Patroclus, in which the words occur: 'The back of Eumelus was warm with their breath', and 'They seemed ever on the point of springing on to (αἰεί ... ἐπιβησομένοισιν ἐΐκτην) the chariot'. The whole of the passage is lucid because no possible or actual occurrence is omitted.

(211) A passage often becomes more lucid when a word is repeated, for example: 'In his lifetime you spoke of him disparagingly; now after his death you write of him disparagingly'. The repetition of the word 'disparagingly' adds lucidity to the attack.

(212) They accuse Ctesias of prolixity, because of his repetitions. It may be that the accusation is often justified, but in many passages his critics do not see how lucid he is. The repetition of the same word often increases the emphasis.

(213) Here is an example. 'Stryangaeus, a Persian, unhorsed a Sacian woman. Women among the Sacae engage in battle like Amazons. When he saw the youthful beauty of the Sacian woman he allowed her to escape. After this, when peace was made, he wooed the woman, but was rejected. He then resolved to starve himself to death, but he first wrote a reproachful letter to the woman couched in the following terms: "I saved your life; yes, you were saved through me. Yet I have perished through you".'

(214) Here a critic who makes a merit of terseness might object to the useless repetition of 'I saved you', and 'You were saved through me', since the two expressions have the same meaning. Yet if you remove either you will rob the passage of its lucidity and consequent pathos. The expression which follows, 'I have perished' instead of 'I am perishing', adds to the lucidity by the use of a past tense. What has taken place is more impressive than what is about to take place.

(215) Generally speaking, this poet—and Ctesias well deserves the title of poet—is a master of lucidity in all his writings.

(216) Another example may be added. It is right not to announce an event abruptly, but by degrees, keeping the hearer in suspense and compelling him to share our anxiety. This is what Ctesias does in announcing Cyrus's death. The messenger comes to Parysatis and does not at once tell her that Cyrus is dead. This would be what is called barbaric brutality. First he announces his victory, and she is glad and full of excitement. Then she asks how the king fares. He announces that he has escaped. She replies: 'He has Tissaphernes to thank for this'. Again she asks: 'Where is Cyrus now?' The messenger replies: 'He is where all brave men should camp'. Little by little he proceeds, and by degrees he breaks the news. The writer thus gives an expressive and lucid picture of the messenger's reluctance to announce the disaster, and unites the mother and the reader in a common distress.

(217) Lucidity is obtained also by narrating circumstances connected with the story. For example, in describing a rustic's approach, a writer said: 'From afar the clatter of his feet was heard, as he came near'. This sentence suggests a person not walking, but pounding the ground.

(218) Similar to this is Plato's description of Hippocrates: 'He blushed. Day was now dawning and it betrayed him'. Any one can see how lucid this passage is. The lucidity is caused by the thought bestowed on the narrative, and the reminder that Hippocrates' visit was at night.

(219) Harshness of sound is often used. For example, the passage in Homer, 'He smote them, and their

brains, etc.', and the passage, 'Upward and downward, etc.'. By the harsh sound he suggests the uneven ground. Imitation is always lucid.

(220) Coined words are lucid as they are imitative. For example, 'lapping'. If Homer had said 'drinking', he would not have represented the drinking of dogs, and there would have been nothing lucid. But the combination of the two words λάπτοντες (lapping) γλώσσῃσι (with their tongues) gives a still greater lucidity. This, then, will suffice for a brief sketch of lucidity.

(221) The persuasive style requires two qualities: clearness and simplicity. If it is lacking in either of these it fails to persuade. We must aim at a diction which is neither overladen nor ponderous if we wish to persuade; a diction, too, with a steady rhythm and no suggestion of metre.

(222) These are the qualities needed for a persuasive style. Theophrastus adds that every detail must not be described at length, but some points must be left to the intelligence and elaboration of the hearer. When he thinks of the points which you have omitted, he becomes not only a hearer, but a witness and a very partial witness, too. He thinks that he is clever, thanks to your action in giving him an opportunity to use his intelligence. To press home every detail, as though your hearer were a fool, seems like casting a slur on his intelligence.

(223) Since the epistolary style needs to be plain, I will also speak about this. Artemon, who edited Aristotle's letters, says that dialogue and letters should be written in the same manner. A letter, he says, is, as it were, the reverse side of a dialogue.

(224) There is truth, it may be, in what he says, but not the whole truth. A letter requires more elaboration

than a dialogue. The dialogue aims at extemporizing, but the letter is sent as a kind of literary present.

(225) Who would ever talk to a friend in the style in which Aristotle writes to Antipater on behalf of the aged exile? He says: 'If he is wandering in exile over the whole world, without hope of being recalled, no one surely will blame such men if they wish to descend to the kingdom of Hades'. He who talks in this style suggests a man who is trying to show off and not one who is merely talking.

(226) Frequent breaks are not suitable to letters. The break in writing causes obscurity, and imitation is not so much a characteristic of writing as of oratory. Compare the passage in the *Euthydemus*: 'Who was he, Socrates, with whom you were talking yesterday in the Lyceum? There was a great crowd round you and your friends'. A little later, he adds: 'I think that the man you were talking with was a stranger. Tell me, who was he?' All such imitative style is suited to drama, but not to letters.

(227) The letter should, to a large extent, be expressive of character, like the dialogue. Every one in writing a letter is giving, as it were, a picture of his own soul. Indeed, all literary composition enables the reader to see the character of the writer, but none does this so clearly as the letter.

(228) The length of the letter, no less than its diction, requires regulation. Excessively long letters and those, too, which are too ponderous in style, are in no true sense letters, but treatises with an epistolary heading and subscription added. Such as these are many of Plato's letters and the one letter of Thucydides.

(229) A letter should have a looser order. It is ridiculous to write in periods, as if you were composing not a letter but the speech of a prosecuting counsel.

It is not merely ridiculous to labour thus in letters, but unfriendly. Friendship expects us to 'call a spade a spade', as the proverb says.

(230) We must realize that there is not only a certain diction, but certain matter which is appropriate to letters. At any rate, Aristotle, who seems more than any one to have been a master of the epistolary style, says: 'I am not writing to you about this; it is no topic for a letter'.

(231) If any one should use a letter to discuss tricks of logic, or natural history, he would be writing indeed, but not writing a letter. A letter is intended to be a brief display of kindliness; it deals with simple topics, and is expressed in simple words.

(232) Its beauty consists of kindly admonitions, with a frequent mixture of proverbs. This should be the only bit of philosophy it contains, because a proverb is a popular commonplace. But the composer of maxims or the preacher of sermons requires the assistance, not of a letter, but of a pulpit.

(233) Aristotle, however, on occasions in his letters, uses logical proofs. For example, he tries to prove that it is right to show good treatment alike to large and small cities, and he says: 'The Gods in both are equal. Therefore, since the Graces are Gods, you must find room for them equally in both'. His contention is quite epistolary in character, and so is his method of proof.

(234) There are occasions when we address letters to states and to kings. Such letters as these may be allowed a somewhat elevated style. It is right to adapt ourselves to the person to whom we are writing. The elevation, however, should not go so far as to convert the letter into a treatise, like the letter of Aristotle to Alexander, or that of Plato to Dion's friends.

(235) To sum up, a letter should in its style contain

a blend of these two qualities, the graceful and the plain. I have spoken enough about the epistolary style and the plain style.

(236) There is a perversion corresponding to the plain style, which is called arid. This, too, falls under three headings: first, the sense, as when a writer said of Xerxes: 'Xerxes came to the coast with all his men'. Here he belittled the scene. He should have said: 'He came with the whole of Asia', but he said 'with all his men'.

(237) Secondly, aridity arises from the diction, when any one describes an important situation in feeble words, as when Theodorus of Gadara describes the battle of Salamis; and someone else said of the tyrant Phalaris: 'In certain matters Phalaris annoyed the men of Acragas'. So fierce a conflict and so savage a tyrant ought not to have been described by the words 'certain matters' and 'annoyed', but in stately language appropriate to the subject-matter.

(238) Thirdly, aridity depends on the composition. This happens when there are numerous short phrases, as in the aphorisms: 'Life is short; art is long; time is fleeting; effort is elusive'. It happens also when in an important theme the member is short and not continuous. An example of this is when someone was condemning Aristeides for not taking part in the battle of Salamis, and said, 'Demeter came and fought with us; but Aristeides, no!' Such an abrupt ending is unseemly and ill-placed. It is legitimate, however, to use such abrupt clauses in other contexts.

(239) It often happens that the idea itself is frigid, and what we now call 'affected', while the composition is abrupt, and attempts to conceal the unattractiveness of the idea. For example, a certain writer, referring to the man who caressed his wife when she was dead,

said, 'He caresses her no more'. The idea is clear, even to the blind, as the proverb says, but the concise diction hides to some extent the unattractiveness of the story, and produces a style now known as 'affected aridity', a fault compounded of two others, affectation which is due to the story, and aridity which is due to the style.

V

(240) We now come to the powerful style. From what has been already said it will be clear that this style, like those that have been already described, depends upon three qualities. Some events suggest power by their innate character, so that those who describe them seem powerful, even though there is no power in their language. For example, Theopompus describes the flute-girls in the Peiraeus and the brothels, and those who pipe and sing and dance. In spite of the feebleness of his description, he seems powerful.

(241) In the matter of composition, this style would be produced by substituting short clauses for members. Prolixity destroys vehemence; when much is expressed in a small compass, there is an increase of power. An example is the message of the Lacedemonians to Philip, 'Dionysius in Corinth'. If they had expanded it and said, 'Dionysius has been banished from his throne and is earning a beggarly living in Corinth as a schoolmaster', the message would have been rather a narrative than a gibe.

(242) In all their conversation the Lacedemonians were naturally concise. A brief authoritative statement is more powerful; lengthy utterance resembles entreaty and prayer.

(243) Symbolic utterances are powerful, because they resemble short statements. From a short statement much can be inferred, and the same applies to symbolic remarks. For example, the allegorical saying: 'The cicalas shall sing to you from the ground', is more powerful expressed in this way than if they had said simply: 'Your trees shall be cut down'.

(244) The periods must be abridged at the end. The periodic style is powerful, but a loose style is indicative of simplicity and good nature, as the style of the ancients always was. The ancients were distinguished by simplicity.

(245) In the powerful style the old-fashioned pattern of character and rhythm must be avoided—especially if we aim at the powerful style which is now in vogue. In periods, cadences like the following, 'I complied with my clients' wish to plead their cause to the best of my powers', are most in keeping with the rhythm which I have described.

(246) Vehemence, too, creates a kind of power in composition. Roughness of sound also in many cases indicates power, like the effect of uneven words. An example is seen in the passage of Demosthenes: 'He has robbed you of the power to give—you of your right'.

(247) Antithetical and parallel clauses in periods must be avoided. They are bombastic and not powerful; they often create frigidity instead of power; for example, when Theopompus was denouncing Philip's friends he weakened the power of his words by the following antithesis: 'Men-slayers they were by nature and men-defilers by habit'. The listener finds his mind fixed on the artificial style, which is also bad art, and loses all sense of indignation.

(248) Often the very nature of the subject will compel

us to compose sentences which are both rounded and powerful. The following passage from Demosthenes is an example: 'If one of them had been convicted, you would not have made these proposals. If, therefore, you are now convicted, no one else will make such proposals'. The very subject-matter and order of the words without doubt gave rise to the structure which grew out of it, and no violence could easily have altered its construction. There are many facts which guide our composition, and we are impelled by our very subject, just like men racing down an incline.

(249) It conduces to power to place the strongest thought at the end; whatever is buried in the middle of the sentence loses its force. Antisthenes illustrates this: 'Oft will a man cause pain when out from brushwood he arises'.

If the order is changed and the passage runs thus: 'Oft arising from brushwood a man will cause pain', although the words are the same, the effect will be different.

(250) Antithesis, which I criticized in Theopompus, is no less out of place in Demosthenes, as, for example, when he says: 'You were initiating; I was the initiate. You were the master, I the scholar. You were acting a minor part; I was a spectator. You were driven off the stage; I was hissing'. This passage seems affected because of the contrasts; it is more like a jest than a denunciation.

(251) Powerful style is helped by a succession of periods, although this is not advisable in other styles. Periods succeeding one another will suggest lines of verse recited one after another—and powerful verse, too, like choliambics.

(252) However, these successive periods must also be short—consisting of about two members. If they

consist of many more they will make the passage beautiful rather than powerful.

(253) For this reason conciseness helps this style; as aposiopesis will often add to the power, as when Demosthenes says: 'For my part I—but I do not wish to say anything disagreeable. My opponent has an advantage over me in his accusation'. By such an eloquent pause the sentence is almost more powerful than anything he might have said.

(254) And in truth ambiguity may often add strength. An idea suggested is more weighty: simplicity of statement excites contempt.

(255) Sometimes harshness of language adds power, especially when the underlying theme requires it—as in Homer:

Τρῶες δ' ἐρρίγησαν, ὅπως ἴδον αἰόλον ὄφιν

(The Trojans trembled when they saw the writhing
   snake).

He could have saved his metre, and at the same time have spoken more melodiously, by a slight change:

Τρῶες δ' ἐρρίγησαν, ὅπως ὄφιν αἰόλον εἶδον.

But then neither poet nor snake would have created so powerful an impression.

(256) Following this example we may make many similar experimental changes in order. Instead of πάντα ἂν ἔγραψεν, we may write ἔγραψεν ἄν, and for οὐ παρεγένετο we may substitute παρεγένετο οὐχί.

(257) We may sometimes end a sentence with the conjunctions δέ or τε, although we are warned to avoid such an ending. Yet it might be useful in many passages, for example: 'He did not speak well of him, much though he deserved it; he insulted him, rather' (ἠτίμασε δέ), and in the expression, Σχοῖνόν τε Σκῶλόν τε. In Homer stateliness is caused by ending with conjunctions.

(258) Power would be sometimes added by composing the following type of sentence: 'In his recklessness and impiety he overturned everything, sacred and profane alike' (τὰ ἱερά τε τὰ ὅσιά τε). Generally speaking, smoothness and euphony belong to the polished and not to the powerful style; and these two styles are regarded as extreme opposites.

(259) And yet it often happens that a mixture of playfulness gives an appearance of power—for example, in comedies and the usual style of the Cynics. The line of Crates is also an instance: 'A dwarfed land lies in the midst of the wine-dark vapour'.

(260) There is also the remark of Diogenes at Olympia when, at the end of the hoplites' race, he ran up and proclaimed himself as victor at Olympia over all mankind—in personal character. His words evoke at once laughter and admiration. There is a subtle pungency about the words.

(261) There is also his remark to the handsome youth. Diogenes was wrestling with a handsome boy and accidentally assumed an indecent position. The boy was frightened and shrank back, but Diogenes said: 'Don't be afraid, dear boy. I am no match for you in *that*'. The readiness of his reply causes laughter; and there was strength in the hidden emphasis. To sum up, a speech of a Cynic always suggests a dog which bites while it wags its tail.

(262) Orators will adopt this method on occasions, and have done so. Such was Lysias' remark to the old woman's suitor: 'It is easier to count her teeth than her fingers'. He here depicts the old woman in the strongest and most amusing way. Homer's sentence has already been quoted: 'Noman I will eat last of all'.

(263) I will now describe how power may be derived from the use of figures. It comes from the figure which

is called 'passing over'. For example: 'Olynthus and Methone and Apollonia and thirty-two cities in Thrace I pass over'. In this sentence he has actually said all he wanted, and he pretends to have passed them by as though he had more powerful accusations to make.

(264) Aposiopesis, a figure already mentioned, partakes of the same character and adds strength to the expression.

(265) There is a figure of thought which helps in strengthening the language. It is called 'prospopoeia'. Here is an example: 'Imagine that your ancestors, or Hellas or your country, in the form of a woman, should reproach you in these words'.

(266) This figure is used in Pericles' funeral oration, when he says: 'My sons,—that ye are sprung from noble fathers, etc.'. He is not speaking in his own person, but in that of their fathers. The argument comes with greater appeal and power by being thus personified. The whole passage assumes a dramatic character.

(267) The forms of thought and figures of speech may be adopted as I have described them. All my quotations will serve to illustrate them. The more cleverly you choose the figures of speech, the more powerful you can make your language. There is the figure of 'repetition': 'Thebes, Thebes, our near neighbour, has been plucked out from the midst of Hellas'. The repetition of the name adds force.

(268) There is also the figure called 'anaphora'. For example: 'Against thyself dost thou call him; against the laws dost thou call him; against the democracy dost thou call him'. Here the figure used is threefold. There is 'anaphora', as I have said, because the same word is repeated at the opening of each clause; there is 'asyndeton', because the sentence employs no conjunctions; and there is 'homoioteleuton', because the

phrase, 'dost thou call him', constantly appears at the end. Power comes from the combination of the three. If you paraphrase it thus: 'Against thyself and the laws and the democracy dost thou call him', you will rob the passage alike of the figures and of its power.

(269) You must know that disjunction more than any figure produces power. For example: 'He walks through the assembly, puffing out his cheeks, knitting his brows, keeping step with Pythocles'. If these sentences were joined by conjunctions, they would become tamer.

(270) We can use also the figure called 'climax'. Demosthenes says: 'I did not speak without proposing it; I did not propose it without going on the embassy; I did not go on the embassy without persuading the Thebans'. The language may be compared to one mounting from height to height. If you spoke the sentence thus: 'I spoke and made the proposal, and went on the embassy and persuaded the Thebans', you would make a bare narration devoid of all power.

(271) To sum up, the figures of style aid the speaker in delivery and debating power; in particular they produce an abrupt style which adds strength. Enough, then, has been said about the figures.

(272) We may adopt every form of diction that has been mentioned in reference to the stately style—only with a different end in view. Metaphorical expressions often add power, for example: 'To Python waxing bold and rushing down on you in full stream'.

(273) The use of similes will serve the same purpose as in Demosthenes: 'This decree caused the danger which then was threatening the state to pass by like a cloud'.

(274) Parabolic expressions are unsuited to the powerful style because of their length, for example: 'Like a well-bred but untrained hound which heedlessly attacks a boar'. Such sentences show beauty and

precision, but strength requires something vigorous and terse, and is like boxers engaging in close contact.

(275) Power is also gained by a compound word, as in those powerful words coined by usage, for example, 'earth-beaten' or 'sideway-stricken', and other similar words. The orators will furnish many such examples.

(276) We must make an effort to adapt the words to the deeds. We say of one who acted with un-principled violence, 'he forced his way through'; of one who acted with undisguised and reckless violence, 'he hewed his way through; he brushed every obstacle aside'; of one who acted in a crafty and furtive manner, 'he bored a way through; he wormed his way in'. Other words we apply that suit our matter.

(277) The assumption of exalted language adds both stateliness and power; for example: 'You ought not to [1] speak, Aeschines, without holding out your palm; but you ought to have gone as an ambassador without holding out your palm'.

(278) So in the passage which begins: 'But in annexing Euboea'. The elevation of language did not aim at investing the language with stateliness, but with power. This happens when at the height of our rhetoric we are denouncing an opponent. The former passage is a denunciation of Aeschines and the latter of Philip.

(279) A sentence gains power when we ask our hearers questions and do not reveal the answer. 'But in annexing Euboea, and planning a base of attack against Attica, was he acting wrongly in so doing? was he violating the peace, or not?' He brings his hearer, as it were, into a quandary as though he were being cross-questioned and could not supply an answer. If the passage had been delivered thus: 'He was acting

---

[1] An eloquent speaker holds out his hand as an oratorical gesture; an incorruptible ambassador keeps his hand hidden.

wrongly and violating the peace', it would have resembled a plain statement, not a cross-examination.

(280) The figure known as 'lingering' is a figure which exceeds the bare facts of the case, and it will greatly enhance the power of the sentence. An example occurs in Demosthenes: 'Athenians, a terrible scourge has befallen Hellas'.[1] The passage, thus shortened, would have lost power.

(281) The figure called 'euphemism' may, perhaps, belong to the powerful style, the figure, that is, which makes ill-omened words sound good-omened, and impious words sound pious. The citizen, for example, who advocated melting down the golden images of Victory and using the money for the war did not say bluntly: 'Let us cut the statues to pieces for the war'. This would have sounded like an ill-omened proposal and blasphemous to the goddess. He used an expression of better omen, and said: 'We will invoke the statues of Victory to help us in the war'. So expressed, it did not sound like cutting the statues to pieces, but enlisting them as allies.

(282) The sayings of Demades, too, possess power, although their expression sounds peculiar and unusual. Their power arises partly from their significance and partly from their allegorical form, and lastly from their exaggerated character.

(283) This is an example: 'Alexander is not dead, Athenians. If he were, the whole world would smell the corpse'. The use of the word 'smell' for 'perceive' involves both allegory and exaggeration. The fact that the world perceived it signifies Alexander's strength, and at the same time the sentence has a startling effect, which is due to a combination of three causes. Everything that startles is powerful, because it creates fear.

[1] Demosthenes *Falsa leg.* 259.   The original passage elaborates the sentence.   The elaboration forms the 'lingering'.

(284) To the same class belong these sayings: 'It was not I who drafted this decree, but the war, using Alexander's spear as a pen', and 'The power of Macedon, now that it has lost Alexander, resembles the Cyclops when he had lost his eye.'

(285) In another place he says: 'A city—no longer the naval power that it was in the time of our ancestors, but an aged woman wearing slippers and supping gruel'. The term 'aged woman' is allegorical, and is substituted for the epithets 'weak' or 'failing'; at the same time it gives an exaggerated description of the city's listlessness. The expression 'supping gruel' alludes to the fact that it was wasting its war funds at that time in feasts and banquets.

(286) These quotations are enough to indicate the power of Demades' style. And yet the style is dangerous and cannot be imitated closely. It contains a poetical element, if allegory and hyperbole and significance are poetical. But its poetry is mixed with comedy.

(287) The so-called 'figured language' is employed by modern orators to an absurd degree, and at the same time it is combined with a base and suggestive significance. The true 'figured language' is combined with tact and care.

(288) An example of tact is seen when Plato wished to censure Aristippus and Cleombrotus who were feasting in Aegina, when Socrates had been lying in prison at Athens for a number of days, and who made no effort to release their friend and master, although they were scarcely more than twenty miles from Athens. Plato does not state all these facts in so many words. To do so would have been sheer abuse. Phaedo was asked for a list of those who were present with Socrates, and when he had given all the names, he was asked again whether Aristippus and Cleombrotus were there.

He replied, 'No; they were in Aegina'. The point of all that precedes is revealed in the words, 'they were in Aegina'. The argument seems greatly strengthened as the facts themselves reveal the scandal, which is not stated in so many words. Though it might, perhaps, have been quite safe to censure Aristippus and his friends openly, Plato preferred to do so in a figurative manner.

(289) Often when we converse with a tyrant or any presumptuous person, and wish to reproach them, we are driven to use a figure of speech. Demetrius of Phalerum, for example, was addressing the Macedonian Craterus, who was sitting on a raised golden throne and wearing a purple cloak, and was receiving the Greek embassies with an air of haughtiness, and he disguised his censure in figurative language: 'We too once received these men as ambassadors, including Craterus yonder'. By the pointed use of the word 'yonder', all the insolent behaviour of Craterus is clearly censured under a figure of language.

(290) To the same class belongs the retort of Plato to Dionysius, who had both broken a promise and denied that he had made it. 'I, Plato, never promised you anything: but you, by Heaven!' His falsehood is thus brought home to him, and at the same time the language is stately and careful.

(291) Often, however, writers use ambiguities. If any one wishes to follow this example and to convey censure, he will find an example in the passage of Aeschines which refers to Telauges. Almost the whole of this narrative about Telauges will leave the reader wondering whether it is genuine admiration or mockery. Such a type of language is ambiguous, and yet though not actual irony it still leaves a kind of ironical impression.

(292) There are other occasions on which figures may be used. Inasmuch as lords and ladies do not welcome

the recital of their own misdeeds, when we admonish
them not to fall into error we shall not speak directly,
but we shall perhaps criticize others who have committed like errors; for example, in addressing the tyrant
Dionysius we shall denounce the tyrant Phalaris and
his cruel deeds. Or we shall praise others whose conduct has been of the opposite kind, for example, Gelo
or Hiero, who were like fathers and instructors of Sicily.
By listening he is admonished without being censured,
and he is led to imitate Gelo who wins such praise, and
he aims at deserving it himself.

(293) Often similar caution must be practised in the
presence of tyrants. For example, Philip, who had
only one eye, resented any reference to Cyclops in his
presence, or reference to an eye at all. Hermeias, too,
the ruler of Artaneus, whose rule is said to have been
gentle in all respects, could not endure any one to refer
to a knife, or to cutting or amputation, because he was
a eunuch. I mention these instances, because I want
to indicate the character of tyrants, and to show that
they particularly call for careful language, which is
called 'figured language'.

(294) And yet great and strong democracies often
call for the same kind of language as tyrants. For
example, there was the democracy of Athens which was
the ruler of Hellas and contained flatterers like a Cleon
or a Cleophon. To flatter is degrading, to censure is
dangerous; the middle course is best, to adopt 'figured
language'.

(295) Sometimes we shall praise a man who falls
into error, not for his errors, but for avoiding them; for
example, we shall praise the quick-tempered man for
winning praise yesterday for his leniency to such or
such a man's offences, and for living a life among his
fellow citizens which is a pattern to them. Every man

finds pleasure in imitating his own qualities, and wishes to add praise to praise, or rather to acquire one consistent record of praise.

(296) To sum up, as out of the same wax one man models a hound, another an ox, and another a horse, so different effects can be produced by the same subject-matter. One man speaks in open disapproval and says: 'Men leave their money to their children, but with the money they do not leave knowledge how to use the legacy'. This kind of comment is called Aristippian. Another will put forward the same idea in the form of a suggestion, as Xenophon generally does: 'It is right not only to leave money to one's children, but also knowledge how to use it'.

(297) There is also the so-called Socratic method, which Aeschines and Plato especially seem to imitate. This will transform the incident quoted into a question, much as follows: 'My boy, how much money did your father leave you? Was it a large sum that could not easily be counted?'

'It was a large sum, Socrates.'

'Did he then also leave you knowledge how to use it?'

At one and the same time he artfully leads the boy into a quandary, and reminds him of his ignorance, and induces him to seek instruction. All this effect is produced with due regard to sound morals and good taste, and not, as they say, with Scythian brusqueness.

(298) Such discourses as these when first invented met with much success; or rather they startled people by their suggestive and lucid character and their impressive admonitions. Let this, then, suffice about models of style and figured language.

(299) Smoothness of composition, which is used chiefly by the pupils of Isocrates who avoided a combination of vowel sounds, is not very suitable to powerful

language. Often a more powerful effect could be produced by their actual concurrence. For example: 'When the Phocian war was declared originally, in no sense through my agency; I indeed as yet had no share in public life'. If the order of the sentence were changed: 'When the Phocian war, through no fault of mine, was originally declared, for I had as yet no share in public life', a great deal of power would be lost; for often the very noise of clashing vowels will increase power.

(300) An unpremeditated and spontaneous utterance will create a certain kind of power, especially when we represent ourselves as angry or the victims of injustice. An elaborate smoothness and rhythmical style is not a sign of anger, but of playfulness and a desire to display our skill.

(301) I have said that a loose style produces power; the same effect will be created by a generally loose diction. An example can be seen in Hipponax. When he wanted to abuse his enemies, he shattered his metre, and made his language halt instead of standing erect, and destroyed its rhythm. He thereby produced a style which was strong and abusive. A rhythmical and pleasing style would adapt itself better to eulogy than to denunciation. This, then, will suffice for the collision of vowels.

(302) Corresponding to the powerful style there is, as you would expect, a perverted style which is called 'disagreeable'. It depends upon the subject-matter, when a speaker openly describes incidents which are degrading and should never be mentioned. For example, the accuser of Timandra for her immoral life defiled the court with a description of her bowl and her appliances, and her rush mat, and many other objectionable details of a courtesan's life.

(303) Composition seems disagreeable if it has a disjointed appearance, like the remark, 'Since such and such is the case, slay them,'—or when the members have no connection with one another, but are like broken fragments. Long continuous periods which take away the speaker's breath are not only wearisome but repellent.

(304) Often pleasing objects lose their charm by a wrong choice of words. When Cleitarchus was describing a wasp, a creature very like a bee, he said: 'It ravages the hillside; it rushes into the hollow oaks'. He might have been describing a wild bull or the Erymanthian boar, instead of a kind of bee. His language, therefore, was both disagreeable and frigid. These two defects are in a way closely akin.

LONGINUS ON THE SUBLIME

TRANSLATED BY H. L. HAVELL

I

THE treatise of Caecilius on the Sublime, when, as you remember, my dear Terentian, we examined it together, seemed to us to be beneath the dignity of the whole subject, to fail entirely in seizing the salient points, and to offer little profit (which should be the principal aim of every writer) for the trouble of its perusal. There are two things essential to a technical treatise: the first is to define the subject; the second (I mean second in order, as it is by much the first in importance) to point out how and by what methods we may become masters of it ourselves. And yet Caecilius, while wasting his efforts in a thousand illustrations of the nature of the Sublime, as though here we were quite in the dark, somehow passes by as immaterial the question how we might be able to exalt our own genius to a certain degree of progress in sublimity. However, perhaps it would be fairer to commend this writer's intelligence and zeal in themselves, instead of blaming him for his omissions. And since you have bidden me also to put together, if only for your entertainment, a few notes on the subject of the Sublime, let me see if there is anything in my speculations which promises advantage to men of affairs. In you, dear friend—such is my confidence in your abilities, and such the part which becomes you—I look for a sympathizing and discerning [1] critic of the several parts of my treatise. For that was a just remark of his who pronounced that the points in which we resemble the divine nature are benevolence and love of truth.

[1] Reading φιλοφρονέστατα καὶ ἀληθέστατα.

As I am addressing a person so accomplished in literature, I need only state, without enlarging further on the matter, that the Sublime, wherever it occurs, consists in a certain loftiness and excellence of language, and that it is by this, and this only, that the greatest poets and prose-writers have gained eminence, and won themselves a lasting place in the Temple of Fame. A lofty passage does not convince the reason of the reader, but takes him out of himself. That which is admirable ever confounds our judgment, and eclipses that which is merely reasonable or agreeable. To believe or not is usually in our own power; but the Sublime, acting with an imperious and irresistible force, sways every reader whether he will or no. Skill in invention, lucid arrangement and disposition of facts, are appreciated not by one passage, or by two, but gradually manifest themselves in the general structure of a work; but a sublime thought, if happily timed, illumines [1] an entire subject with the vividness of a lightning-flash, and exhibits the whole power of the orator in a moment of time. Your own experience, I am sure, my dearest Terentian, would enable you to illustrate these and similar points of doctrine.

II

The first question which presents itself for solution is whether there is any art which can teach sublimity or loftiness in writing. For some hold generally that there is mere delusion in attempting to reduce such subjects to technical rules. 'The Sublime', they tell us, 'is born in a man, and not to be acquired by instruction; genius is the only master who can teach it. The

[1] Reading διεφώτισεν.

vigorous products of nature' (such is their view) 'are weakened and in every respect debased, when robbed of their flesh and blood by frigid technicalities'. But I maintain that the truth can be shown to stand otherwise in this matter. Let us look at the case in this way; Nature in her loftier and more passionate moods, while detesting all appearance of restraint, is not wont to show herself utterly wayward and reckless; and though in all cases the vital informing principle is derived from her, yet to determine the right degree and the right moment, and to contribute the precision of practice and experience, is the peculiar province of scientific method. The great passions, when left to their own blind and rash impulses without the control of reason, are in the same danger as a ship let drive at random without ballast. Often they need the spur, but sometimes also the curb. The remark of Demosthenes with regard to human life in general—that the greatest of all blessings is to be fortunate, but next to that and equal in importance is to be well advised—for good fortune is utterly ruined by the absence of good counsel—may be applied to literature, if we substitute genius for fortune, and art for counsel. Then, again (and this is the most important point of all), a writer can only learn from art when he is to abandon himself to the direction of his genius.[1]

These are the considerations which I submit to the unfavourable critic of such useful studies. Perhaps they may induce him to alter his opinion as to the vanity and idleness of our present investigations.

[1] Lit. 'But the most important point of all is that the actual fact that there are some parts of literature which are in the power of natural genius alone, must be learnt from no other source than from art'.

III

... 'And let them check the stove's long
         tongues of fire:
For if I see one tenant of the hearth,
I'll thrust within one curling torrent flame,
And bring that roof in ashes to the ground:
But now not yet is sung my noble lay'.[1]

Such phrases cease to be tragic, and become burlesque
—I mean phrases like 'curling torrent flames' and
'vomiting to heaven', and representing Boreas as a piper,
and so on. Such expressions, and such images, produce
an effect of confusion and obscurity, not of energy; and
if each separately be examined under the light of
criticism, what seemed terrible gradually sinks into
absurdity. Since then, even in tragedy, where the
natural dignity of the subject makes a swelling diction
allowable, we cannot pardon a tasteless grandiloquence,
how much more incongruous must it seem in sober prose!
Hence we laugh at those fine words of Gorgias of Leon-
tini, such as 'Xerxes the Persian Zeus' and 'vultures,
those living tombs', and at certain conceits of Callisthenes
which are high-flown rather than sublime, and at some
in Cleitarchus more ludicrous still—a writer whose
frothy style tempts us to travesty Sophocles and say:
'He blows a little pipe, and blows it ill'. The same
faults may be observed in Amphicrates and Hegesias and
Matris, who in their frequent moments (as they think)
of inspiration, instead of playing the genius are simply
playing the fool.

Speaking generally, it would seem that bombast is one
of the hardest things to avoid in writing. For all those
writers who are ambitious of a lofty style, through dread

[1] Aeschylus in his lost *Oreithyia*.

of being convicted of feebleness and poverty of language, slide by a natural gradation into the opposite extreme. 'Who fails in great endeavour, nobly fails', is their creed. Now bulk, when hollow and affected, is always objectionable, whether in material bodies or in writings, and in danger of producing on us an impression of littleness: 'Nothing', it is said, 'is drier than a man with the dropsy'.

The characteristic, then, of bombast is that it transcends the Sublime: but there is another fault diametrically opposed to grandeur: this is called puerility, and it is the failing of feeble and narrow minds—indeed, the most ignoble of all vices in writing. By puerility we mean a pedantic habit of mind, which by over-elaboration ends in frigidity. Slips of this sort are made by those who, aiming at brilliancy, polish, and especially attractiveness, are landed in paltriness and silly affectation. Closely associated with this is a third sort of vice, in dealing with the passions, which Theodorus used to call false sentiment, meaning by that an ill-timed and empty display of emotion, where no emotion is called for, or of greater emotion than the situation warrants. Thus we often see an author hurried by the tumult of his mind into tedious displays of mere personal feeling which has no connection with the subject. Yet how justly ridiculous must an author appear, whose most violent transports leave his readers quite cold! However, I will dismiss this subject, as I intend to devote a separate work to the treatment of the pathetic in writing.

IV

The last of the faults which I mentioned is frequently observed in Timaeus—I mean the fault of frigidity. In other respects he is an able writer, and sometimes not unsuccessful in the loftier style; a man of wide knowledge, and full of ingenuity; a most bitter critic of the failings of others—but unhappily blind to his own. In his eagerness to be always striking out new thoughts he frequently falls into the most childish absurdities. I will only instance one or two passages, as most of them have been pointed out by Caecilius. Wishing to say something very fine about Alexander the Great he speaks of him as a man 'who annexed the whole of Asia in fewer years than Isocrates spent in writing his panegyric oration in which he urges the Greeks to make war on Persia'. How strange is the comparison of the 'great Emathian conqueror' with an Athenian rhetorician! By this mode of reasoning it is plain that the Spartans were very inferior to Isocrates in courage, since it took them thirty years to conquer Messene, while he finished the composition of this harangue in ten. Observe, too, his language on the Athenians taken in Sicily. 'They paid the penalty for their impious outrage on Hermes in mutilating his statues; and the chief agent in their destruction was one who was descended on his father's side from the injured deity—Hermocrates, son of Hermon'. I wonder, my dearest Terentian, how he omitted to say of the tyrant Dionysius that for his impiety towards Zeus and Herakles he was deprived of his power by Dion and Herakleides. Yet why speak of Timaeus, when even men like Xenophon and Plato— the very demi-gods of literature—though they had sat at the feet of Socrates, sometimes forgot themselves in the pursuit of such paltry conceits. The former, in his account of the Spartan Polity, has these words: 'Their voice you would no more hear than if they were of marble, their gaze is as immovable as if they were cast in bronze; you would deem them more modest than the very maidens in their eyes'.[1] To speak of the pupils of the eyes as 'modest maidens' was a piece of absurdity becoming Amphicrates[2] rather than Xenophon. And then what a strange delusion to suppose that modesty is always without exception expressed in the eye! whereas it is commonly said that there is nothing by which an impudent fellow betrays his character so much as by the expression of his eyes. Thus Achilles addresses Agamemnon in the Iliad as 'drunkard, with eye of dog'.[3] Timaeus, however, with that want of judgment which characterizes plagiarists, could not leave to Xenophon the possession of even this piece of frigidity. In relating how Agathocles carried off his cousin, who was wedded to another man, from the festival of the unveiling, he asks: 'Who could have done such a deed, unless he had harlots instead of maidens in his eyes?' And Plato himself, elsewhere so supreme a master of style, meaning to describe certain recording tablets, says: 'They shall write, and deposit in the temples memorials of cypress wood';[4] and again: 'Then concerning walls, Megillus, I give my vote with Sparta that we should let them lie asleep within the ground, and not awaken them'.[5] And Herodotus falls pretty much under the same censure, when he speaks of beautiful women as 'tortures to the eye',[6] though here there is some excuse, as the speakers in this passage are drunken barbarians. Still, even from dramatic motives, such errors in taste should not be permitted to deface the pages of an immortal work.

---

[1] *Xen. de Rep. Laced.* 3, 5.   [2] C. iii. sect. 2.   [3] *Il.* i. 225.
[4] *Plat. de Legg.* v. 741, C.   [5] Ib. vi. 778, D.   [6] v. 18.

V

Now all these glaring improprieties of language may be traced to one common root—the pursuit of novelty in thought. It is this that has turned the brain of nearly all the learned world of to-day. Human blessings and human ills commonly flow from the same source: and, to apply this principle to literature, those ornaments of style, those sublime and delightful images, which contribute to success, are the foundation and the origin, not only of excellence, but also of failure. It is thus with the figures called transitions, and hyperboles, and the use of plurals for singulars. I shall show presently the dangers which they seem to involve. Our next task, therefore, must be to propose and to settle the question how we may avoid the faults of style related to sublimity.

VI

Our best hope of doing this will be first of all to grasp some definite theory and criterion of the true Sublime. Nevertheless this is a hard matter; for a just judgment of style is the final fruit of long experience; still, I believe that the way I shall indicate will enable us to distinguish between the true and false Sublime, so far as it can be done by rule.

VII

It is proper to observe that in human life nothing is truly great which is despised by all elevated minds. For example, no man of sense can regard wealth, honour, glory, and power, or any of those things which are surrounded by a great external parade of pomp and circumstance, as the highest blessings, seeing that merely to despise such things is a blessing of no common order: certainly those who possess them are admired much less than those who, having the opportunity to acquire them, through greatness of soul neglect it. Now let us apply this principle to the Sublime in poetry or in prose; let us ask in all cases, is it merely a specious sublimity? is this gorgeous exterior a mere false and clumsy pageant, which if laid open will be found to conceal nothing but emptiness? for if so, a noble mind will scorn instead of admiring it. It is natural to us to feel our souls lifted up by the true Sublime, and conceiving a sort of generous exultation to be filled with joy and pride, as though we had ourselves originated the ideas which we read. If then any work, on being repeatedly submitted to the judgment of an acute and cultivated critic, fails to dispose his mind to lofty ideas; if the thoughts which it suggests do not extend beyond what is actually expressed; and if, the longer you read it, the less you think of it—there can be here no true sublimity, when the effect is not sustained beyond the mere act of perusal. But when a passage is pregnant in suggestion, when it is hard, nay impossible, to distract the attention from it, and when it takes a strong and lasting hold on the memory, then we may be sure that we have lighted on the true Sublime. In general we may regard those words as truly noble and sublime which always please and please all readers. For when the same book always produces the same impression on all who read it, whatever be the difference in their pursuits, their manner of life, their aspirations, their ages, or their language, such a harmony of opposites gives irresistible authority to their favourable verdict.

VIII

I shall now proceed to enumerate the five principal sources, as we may call them, from which almost all sublimity is derived, assuming, of course, the preliminary gift on which all these five sources depend, namely, command of language. The first and the most important is (1) grandeur of thought, as I have pointed out elsewhere in my work on Xenophon. The second is (2) a vigorous and spirited treatment of the passions. These two conditions of sublimity depend mainly on natural endowments, whereas those which follow derive assistance from Art. The third is (3) a certain artifice in the employment of figures, which are of two kinds, figures of thought and figures of speech. The fourth is (4) dignified expression, which is subdivided into (a) the proper choice of words, and (b) the use of metaphors and other ornaments of diction. The fifth cause of sublimity, which embraces all those preceding, is (5) majesty and elevation of structure. Let us consider what is involved in each of these five forms separately.

I must first, however, remark that some of these five divisions are omitted by Caecilius; for instance, he says nothing about the passions. Now if he made this omission from a belief that the Sublime and the Pathetic are one and the same thing, holding them to be always coexistent and interdependent, he is in error. Some passions are found which, so far from being lofty, are actually low, such as pity, grief, fear; and conversely, sublimity is often not in the least affecting, as we may see (among innumerable other instances) in those bold expressions of our great poet on the sons of Aloeus:

'Highly they raged
To pile huge Ossa on the Olympian peak,

> And Pelion with all his waving trees
> On Ossa's crest to raise, and climb the sky';

and the yet more tremendous climax:

> 'And now had they accomplished it'.

And in orators, in all passages dealing with panegyric, and in all the more imposing and declamatory places, dignity and sublimity play an indispensable part; but pathos is mostly absent. Hence the most pathetic orators have usually but little skill in panegyric, and conversely those who are powerful in panegyric generally fail in pathos. If, on the other hand, Caecilius supposed that pathos never contributes to sublimity, and this is why he thought it alien to the subject, he is entirely deceived. For I would confidently pronounce that nothing is so conducive to sublimity as an appropriate display of genuine passion, which bursts out with a kind of 'fine madness' and divine inspiration, and falls on our ears like the voice of a god.

IX

I have already said that of all these five conditions of the Sublime the most important is the first, that is, a certain lofty cast of mind. Therefore, although this is a faculty rather natural than acquired, nevertheless it will be well for us in this instance also to train up our souls to sublimity, and make them as it were ever big with noble thoughts. How, it may be asked, is this to be done? I have hinted elsewhere in my writings that sublimity is, so to say, the image of greatness of soul. Hence a thought in its naked simplicity, even though unuttered, is sometimes admirable by the sheer force of its sublimity; for instance, the silence of Ajax in the eleventh Odyssey [1] is great, and grander than anything he could have said. It is absolutely essential, then, first of all to settle the question whence this grandeur of conception arises; and the answer is that true eloquence can be found only in those whose spirit is generous and aspiring. For those whose whole lives are wasted in paltry and illiberal thoughts and habits cannot possibly produce any work worthy of the lasting reverence of mankind. It is only natural that their words should be full of sublimity whose thoughts are full of majesty. Hence sublime thoughts belong properly to the loftiest minds. Such was the reply of Alexander to his general Parmenio, when the latter had observed: 'Were I Alexander, I should have been satisfied'; 'And I, were I Parmenio' . . .

The distance between heaven and earth [2]—a measure, one might say, not less appropriate to Homer's genius than to the stature of his discord. How different is that touch of Hesiod's in his description of sorrow—if the *Shield* is really one of his works: 'rheum from her nostrils flowed' [3]—an image not terrible, but disgusting. Now consider how Homer gives dignity to his divine persons:

'As far as lies his airy ken, who sits
On some tall crag, and scans the wine-dark sea:
So far extends the heavenly coursers' stride'.[4]

He measures their speed by the extent of the whole world—a grand comparison, which might reasonably lead us to remark that if the divine steeds were to take two such leaps in succession, they would find no room in the world for another. Sublime also are the images in the 'Battle of the Gods':

[1] *Od.* xi. 543.   [2] *Il.* iv. 442.
[3] *Scut. Herc.* 267.   [4] *Il.* v. 770.

'A trumpet sound
Rang through the air, and shook the Olympian height;
Then terror seized the monarch of the dead,
And springing from his throne he cried aloud
With fearful voice, lest the earth, rent asunder
By Neptune's mighty arm, forthwith reveal
To mortal and immortal eyes those halls
So drear and dank, which e'en the gods abhor'.[1]

Earth rent from its foundations! Tartarus itself laid bare! The whole world torn asunder and turned upside down! Why, my dear friend, this is a perfect hurly-burly, in which the whole universe, heaven and hell, mortals and immortals, share the conflict and the peril. A terrible picture, certainly, but (unless perhaps it is to be taken allegorically) downright impious, and over-stepping the bounds of decency. It seems to me that the strange medley of wounds, quarrels, revenges, tears, bonds, and other woes which makes up the Homeric tradition of the gods was designed by its author to degrade his deities, as far as possible, into men, and exalt his men into deities—or rather, his gods are worse off than his human characters, since we, when we are unhappy, have a haven from ills in death, while the gods, according to him, not only live for ever, but live for ever in misery. Far to be preferred to this description of the Battle of the Gods are those passages which exhibit the divine nature in its true light, as something spotless, great, and pure, as, for instance, a passage which has often been handled by my predecessors, the lines on Poseidon:

'Mountain and wood and solitary peak,
The ships Achaian, and the towers of Troy,
Trembled beneath the god's immortal feet.

[1] *Il.* xxi. 388; xx. 61.

Over the waves he rode, and round him played,
Lured from the deeps, the ocean's monstrous brood,
With uncouth gambols welcoming their lord:
The charmèd billows parted: on they flew'.[1]

And thus also the lawgiver of the Jews, no ordinary man,
having formed an adequate conception of the Supreme
Being, gave it adequate expression in the opening words
of his 'Laws': 'God said'—what?—'let there be light,
and there was light: let there be land, and there was'.

I trust you will not think me tedious if I quote yet
one more passage from our great poet (referring this
time to human characters) in illustration of the manner
in which he leads us with him to heroic heights.   A
sudden and baffling darkness as of night has overspread
the ranks of his warring Greeks.   Then Ajax in sore
perplexity cries aloud:

'Almighty Sire,
Only from darkness save Achaia's sons;
No more I ask, but give us back the day;
Grant but our sight, and slay us, if thou wilt'.[2]

The feelings are just what we should look for in Ajax.
He does not, you observe, ask for his life—such a request
would have been unworthy of his heroic soul—but finding
himself paralysed by darkness, and prohibited from
employing his valour in any noble action, he chafes
because his arms are idle, and prays for a speedy return
of light.   'At least', he thinks, 'I shall find a warrior's
grave, even though Zeus himself should fight against me'.
In such passages the mind of the poet is swept along in
the whirlwind of the struggle, and, in his own words, he

'Like the fierce war-god, raves, or wasting fire
Through the deep thickets on a mountain-side;
His lips drop foam'.[3]

[1] *Il*. xiii. 18; xx. 60; xiii. 19, 27.   [2] *Il*. xvii. 645.   [3] *Il*. xv. 605.

But there is another and a very interesting aspect of Homer's mind.   When we turn to the Odyssey we find occasion to observe that a great poetical genius in the decline of power which comes with old age naturally leans towards the fabulous.   For it is evident that this work was composed after the Iliad, in proof of which we may mention, among many other indications, the introduction in the Odyssey of the sequel to the story of his heroes' adventures at Troy, as so many additional episodes in the Trojan war, and especially the tribute of sorrow and mourning which is paid in that poem to departed heroes, as if in fulfilment of some previous design.   The Odyssey is, in fact, a sort of epilogue to the Iliad:

> 'There warrior Ajax lies, Achilles there,
> And there Patroclus, godlike counsellor;
> There lies my own dear son'.[1]

And for the same reason, I imagine, whereas in the Iliad, which was written when his genius was in its prime, the whole structure of the poem is founded on action and struggle, in the Odyssey he generally prefers the narrative style, which is proper to old age.   Hence Homer in his Odyssey may be compared to the setting sun: he is still as great as ever, but he has lost his fervent heat.   The strain is now pitched to a lower key than in the 'Tale of Troy divine': we begin to miss that high and equable sublimity which never flags or sinks, that continuous current of moving incidents, those rapid transitions, that force of eloquence, that opulence of imagery which is ever true to Nature.   Like the sea when it retires upon itself and leaves its shores waste and bare, henceforth the tide of sublimity begins to ebb, and draws us away into the dim region of myth and

[1] *Od.* iii. 109.

legend. In saying this I am not forgetting the fine storm-pieces in the Odyssey, the story of the Cyclops,[1] and other striking passages. It is Homer grown old I am discussing, but still it is Homer. Yet in every one of these passages the mythical predominates over the real.

My purpose in making this digression was, as I said, to point out into what trifles the second childhood of genius is too apt to be betrayed; such, I mean, as the bag in which the winds are confined,[2] the tale of Odysseus's comrades being changed by Circe into swine[3] ('whimpering porkers' Zoïlus called them), and how Zeus was fed like a nestling by the doves,[4] and how Odysseus passed ten nights on the shipwreck without food,[5] and the improbable incidents in the slaying of the suitors.[6] When Homer nods like this, we must be content to say that he dreams as Zeus might dream. Another reason for these remarks on the Odsssey is that I wished to make you understand that great poets and prose-writers, after they have lost their power of depicting the passions, turn naturally to the delineation of character. Such, for instance, is the lifelike and characteristic picture of the palace of Odysseus, which may be called a sort of comedy of manners.

X

Let us now consider whether there is anything further which conduces to the Sublime in writing. It is a law of Nature that in all things there are certain constituent parts, coexistent with their substance. It necessarily follows, therefore, that one cause of sublimity is the

[1] *Od.* ix. 182.   [2] *Od.* x. 17.   [3] *Od.* x. 237.
[4] *Od.* xii. 62.   [5] *Od.* xii. 447.   [6] *Od.* xxii. *passim.*

choice of the most striking circumstances involved in
whatever we are describing, and, further, the power of
afterwards combining them into one animate whole.
The reader is attracted partly by the selection of the
incidents, partly by the skill which has welded them
together. For instance, Sappho, in dealing with the
passionate manifestations attending on the frenzy of
lovers, always chooses her strokes from the signs which
she has observed to be actually exhibited in such cases.
But her peculiar excellence lies in the felicity with which
she chooses and unites together the most striking and
powerful features.

> 'I deem that man divinely blest
> Who sits, and, gazing on thy face,
> Hears thee discourse with eloquent lips,
>   And marks thy lovely smile.
> This, this it is that made my heart
> So wildly flutter in my breast;
> Whene'er I look on thee, my voice
>   Falters, and faints, and fails;
> My tongue 's benumbed; a subtle fire
> Through all my body inly steals;
> Mine eyes in darkness reel and swim;
>   Strange murmurs drown my ears;
> With dewy damps my limbs are chilled;
> An icy shiver shakes my frame;
> Paler than ashes grows my cheek;
>   And Death seems nigh at hand'.

Is it not wonderful how at the same moment soul,
body, ears, tongue, eyes, colour, all fail her, and are lost
to her as completely as if they were not her own?
Observe too how her sensations contradict one another
—she freezes, she burns, she raves, she reasons, and all
at the same instant. And this description is designed

to show that she is assailed, not by any particular
emotion, but by a tumult of different emotions. All
these tokens belong to the passion of love; but it is in
the choice, as I said, of the most striking features, and
in the combination of them into one picture, that the
perfection of this Ode of Sappho's lies. Similarly Homer
in his descriptions of tempests always picks out the most
terrific circumstances. The poet of the 'Arimaspeia'
intended the following lines to be grand:

'Herein I find a wonder passing strange,
    That men should make their dwelling on the deep,
Who far from land essaying bold to range
    With anxious heart their toilsome vigils keep;
    Their eyes are fixed on heaven's starry steep;
The ravening billows hunger for their lives;
    And oft each shivering wretch, constrained to weep,
With suppliant hands to move heaven's pity strives,
While many a direful qualm his very vitals rives'.

All must see that there is more of ornament than of
terror in the description. Now let us turn to Homer.
One passage will suffice to show the contrast.

'On them he leaped, as leaps a raging wave,
Child of the winds, under the darkening clouds,
On a swift ship, and buries her in foam;
Then cracks the sail beneath the roaring blast,
And quakes the breathless seamen's shuddering heart
In terror dire: death lours on every wave'.[1]

Aratus has tried to give a new turn to this last thought:

'But one frail timber shields them from their doom',[2]

banishing by this feeble piece of subtlety all the terror
from his description; setting limits, moreover, to the

[1] *Il.* xv. 624.   [2] *Phaenomena*, 299.

peril described by saying 'shields them'; for so long as it shields them it matters not whether the 'timber' be 'frail' or stout. But Homer does not set any fixed limit to the danger, but gives us a vivid picture of men a thousand times on the brink of destruction, every wave threatening them with instant death. Moreover, by his bold and forcible combination of prepositions of opposite meaning he tortures his language to imitate the agony of the scene, the constraint which is put on the words accurately reflecting the anxiety of the sailors' minds, and the diction being stamped, as it were, with the peculiar terror of the situation. Similarly Archilochus in his description of the shipwreck, and similarly Demosthenes when he describes how the news came of the taking of Elatea [1]—'It was evening', etc. Each of these authors fastidiously rejects whatever is not essential to the subject, and in putting together the most vivid features is careful to guard against the interposition of anything frivolous, unbecoming, or tiresome. Such blemishes mar the general effect, and give a patched and gaping appearance to the edifice of sublimity, which ought to be built up in a solid and uniform structure.

XI

Closely associated with the part of our subject we have just treated of is that excellence of writing which is called amplification, when a writer or pleader, whose theme admits of many successive starting-points and pauses, brings on one impressive point after another in a continuous and ascending scale. Now whether this is employed in the treatment of a commonplace, or in the way of exaggeration, whether to place arguments or

[1] *De Cor.* 169.

facts in a strong light, or in the disposition of actions, or of passions—for amplification takes a hundred different shapes—in all cases the orator must be cautioned that none of these methods is complete without the aid of sublimity—unless, indeed, it be our object to excite pity, or to depreciate an opponent's argument. In all other uses of amplification, if you subtract the element of sublimity you will take as it were the soul from the body. No sooner is the support of sublimity removed than the whole becomes lifeless, nerveless, and dull.

There is a difference, however, between the rules I am now giving and those just mentioned. Then I was speaking of the delineation and co-ordination of the principal circumstances. My next task, therefore, must be briefly to define this difference, and with it the general distinction between amplification and sublimity. Our whole discourse will thus gain in clearness.

XII

I must first remark that I am not satisfied with the definition of amplification generally given by authorities on rhetoric. They explain it to be a form of language which invests the subject with a certain grandeur. Yes, but this definition may be applied indifferently to sublimity, pathos, and the use of figurative language, since all these invest the discourse with some sort of grandeur. The difference seems to me to lie in this, that sublimity gives elevation to a subject, while amplification gives extension as well. Thus the sublime is often conveyed in a single thought, but amplification can only subsist with a certain prolixity and diffusiveness. The most general definition of amplification would explain it to consist in the gathering together of all the constituent parts and topics of a subject, emphasizing the argument by repeated insistence, herein differing from proof, that whereas the object of proof is logical demonstration, . . .

Plato, like the sea, pours forth his riches in a copious and expansive flood. Hence the style of the orator, who is the greater master of our emotions, is often, as it were, red-hot and ablaze with passion, whereas Plato, whose strength lay in a sort of weighty and sober magnificence, though never frigid, does not rival the thunders of Demosthenes. And, if a Greek may be allowed to express an opinion on the subject of Latin literature, I think the same difference may be discerned in the grandeur of Cicero as compared with that of his Grecian rival. The sublimity of Demosthenes is generally sudden and abrupt: that of Cicero is equally diffused. Demosthenes is vehement, rapid, vigorous, terrible; he burns and sweeps away all before him; and hence we may liken him to a whirlwind or a thunderbolt: Cicero is like a widespread conflagration, which rolls over and feeds on all around it, whose fire is extensive and burns long, breaking out successively in different places, and finding its fuel now here, now there. Such points, however, I resign to your more competent judgment.

To resume, then, the high-strung sublimity of Demosthenes is appropriate to all cases where it is desired to exaggerate, or to rouse some vehement emotion, and generally when we want to carry away our audience with us. We must employ the diffusive style, on the other hand, when we wish to overpower them with a flood of language. It is suitable, for example, to familiar topics, and to perorations in most cases, and to digressions, and to all descriptive and declamatory passages, and in dealing with history or natural science, and in numerous other cases.

XIII

To return, however, to Plato: how grand he can be with all that gentle and noiseless flow of eloquence you will be reminded by this characteristic passage, which you have read in his *Republic*: 'They, therefore, who have no knowledge of wisdom and virtue, whose lives are passed in feasting and similar joys, are borne downwards, as is but natural, and in this region they wander all their lives; but they never lifted up their eyes nor were borne upwards to the true world above, nor ever tasted of pleasure abiding and unalloyed; but like beasts they ever look downwards, and their heads are bent to the ground, or rather to the table; they feed full their bellies and their lusts, and longing ever more and more for such things they kick and gore one another with horns and hoofs of iron, and slay one another in their insatiable desires'.[1]

We may learn from this author, if we would but observe his example, that there is yet another path besides those mentioned which leads to sublime heights. What path do I mean? The emulous imitation of the great poets and prose-writers of the past. On this mark, dear friend, let us keep our eyes ever steadfastly fixed. Many gather the divine impulse from another's spirit, just as we are told that the Pythian priestess, when she takes her seat on the tripod, where there is said to be a rent in the ground breathing upwards a heavenly emanation, straightway conceives from that source the godlike gift of prophecy, and utters her inspired oracles; so likewise from the mighty genius of the great writers of antiquity there is carried into the souls of their rivals, as from a fount of inspiration, an effluence which breathes upon them until, even though their natural temper be

[1] *Rep.* ix. 586, A.

but cold, they share the sublime enthusiasm of others. Thus Homer's name is associated with a numerous band of illustrious disciples—not only Herodotus, but Stesichorus before him, and the great Archilochus, and above all Plato, who from the great fountain-head of Homer's genius drew into himself innumerable tributary streams. Perhaps it would have been necessary to illustrate this point, had not Ammonius and his school already classified and noted down the various examples. Now what I am speaking of is not plagiarism, but resembles the process of copying from fair forms or statues or works of skilled labour. Nor in my opinion would so many fair flowers of imagery have bloomed among the philosophical dogmas of Plato, nor would he have risen so often to the language and topics of poetry, had he not engaged heart and soul in a contest for precedence with Homer, like a young champion entering the lists against a veteran. It may be that he showed too ambitious a spirit in venturing on such a duel; but nevertheless it was not without advantage to him: 'For strife like this', as Hesiod says, 'is good for men'.[1] And where shall we find a more glorious arena or a nobler crown than here, where even defeat at the hands of our predecessors is not ignoble?

XIV

Therefore it is good for us also, when we are labouring on some subject which demands a lofty and majestic style, to imagine to ourselves how Homer might have expressed this or that, or how Plato or Demosthenes would have clothed it with sublimity, or, in history, Thucydides. For by our fixing an eye of rivalry on those high examples they will become like beacons to

[1] *Opp.* 29.

guide us, and will perhaps lift up our souls to the fullness of the stature we conceive. And it would be still better should we try to realize this further thought, How would Homer, had he been here, or how would Demosthenes, have listened to what I have written, or how would they have been affected by it? For what higher incentive to exertion could a writer have than to imagine such judges or such an audience of his works, and to give an account of his writings with heroes like these to criticize and look on? Yet more inspiring would be the thought, With what feelings will future ages through all time read these my works? If this should awaken a fear in any writer that he will not be intelligible to his contemporaries it will necessarily follow that the conceptions of his mind will be crude, maimed, and abortive, and lacking that ripe perfection which alone can win the applause of ages to come.

XV

The dignity, grandeur, and energy of a style largely depend on a proper employment of images, a term which I prefer to that usually given.[1] The term image in its most general acceptation includes every thought, howsoever presented, which issues in speech. But the term is now generally confined to those cases when he who is speaking, by reason of the rapt and excited state of his feelings, imagines himself to see what he is talking about, and produces a similar illusion in his hearers. Poets and orators both employ images, but with a very different object, as you are well aware. The poetical image is designed to astound; the oratorical image to give perspicuity. Both, however, seek to work on the emotions.

---

[1] εἰδωλοποιΐαι, 'fictions of the imagination', Hickie.

'Mother, I pray thee, set not thou upon me
  Those maids with bloody face and serpent hair:
  See, see, they come, they're here, they spring upon me!'[1]

And again:

'Ah, ah, she'll slay me! whither shall I fly?'[2]

The poet when he wrote like this saw the Erinyes with
his own eyes, and he almost compels his readers to see
them too. Euripides found his chief delight in the
labour of giving tragic expression to these two passions
of madness and love, showing here a real mastery which
I cannot think he exhibited elsewhere. Still, he is by
no means diffident in venturing on other fields of the
imagination. His genius was far from being of the
highest order, but by taking pains he often raises himself
to a tragic elevation. In his sublimer moments he
generally reminds us of Homer's description of the lion:

'With tail he lashes both his flanks and sides,
  And spurs himself to battle'.[3]

Take, for instance, that passage in which Helios, in
handing the reins to his son, says:

'Drive on, but shun the burning Libyan tract;
  The hot dry air will let thine axle down:
  Toward the seven Pleiades keep thy steadfast way'.

And then:

'This said, his son undaunted snatched the reins,
  Then smote the winged coursers' sides: they bound
  Forth on the void and cavernous vault of air.
  His father mounts another steed, and rides
  With warning voice guiding his son. "Drive there!
  Turn, turn thy car this way"'.[4]

[1] Eur. *Orest.* 255.   [2] *Iph. Taur.* 291.   [3] *Il.* xx. 170.
[4] Eur. *Phaet.*

May we not say that the spirit of the poet mounts the chariot with his hero, and accompanies the winged steeds in their perilous flight? Were it not so—had not his imagination soared side by side with them in that celestial passage—he would never have conceived so vivid an image. Similar is that passage in his *Cassandra*, beginning

'Ye Trojans, lovers of the steed'.[1]

Aeschylus is especially bold in forming images suited to his heroic themes: as when he says of his 'Seven against Thebes':

'Seven mighty men, and valiant captains, slew
Over an iron-bound shield a bull, then dipped
Their fingers in the blood, and all invoked
Ares, Enyo, and death-dealing Flight
In witness of their oaths',[2]

and describes how they all mutually pledged themselves without flinching to die. Sometimes, however, his thoughts are unshapen, and as it were rough-hewn and rugged. Not observing this, Euripides, from too blind a rivalry, sometimes falls under the same censure. Aeschylus with a strange violence of language represents the palace of Lycurgus as *possessed* at the appearance of Dionysus:

'The halls with rapture thrill, the roof's inspired'.[3]

Here Euripides, in borrowing the image, softens its extravagance:[4]

'And all the mountain felt the god'.[5]

[1] Perhaps from the lost *Alexander* (Jahn).
[2] *Sept. c. Th.* 42.   [3] Aesch. *Lycurg.*
[4] Lit 'Giving it a different flavour', as Arist. *Poet.*, ἡδυσμένῳ λόγῳ χωρὶς ἑκάστῳ τῶν εἰδῶν, ii. 10.   [5] *Bacch.* 726.

Sophocles has also shown himself a great master of the imagination in the scene in which the dying Oedipus prepares himself for burial in the midst of a tempest,[1] and where he tells how Achilles appeared to the Greeks over his tomb just as they were putting out to sea on their departure from Troy.[2]   This last scene has also been delineated by Simonides with a vividness which leaves him inferior to none.   But it would be an endless task to cite all possible examples.

To return, then,[3] in poetry, as I observed, a certain mythical exaggeration is allowable, transcending altogether mere logical credence.   But the chief beauties of an oratorical image are its energy and reality.   Such digressions become offensive and monstrous when the language is cast in a poetical and fabulous mould, and runs into all sorts of impossibilities.   Thus much may be learnt from the great orators of our own day, when they tell us in tragic tones that they see the Furies[4]— good people, can't they understand that when Orestes cries out:

'Off, off, I say!   I know thee who thou art,
   One of the fiends that haunt me: I feel thine arms
   About me cast, to drag me down to hell',[5]

these are the hallucinations of a madman?

Wherein, then, lies the force of an oratorical image? Doubtless in adding energy and passion in a hundred different ways to a speech; but especially in this, that when it is mingled with the practical, argumentative parts of an oration, it does not merely convince the hearer, but enthralls him.   Such is the effect of those words of Demosthenes:[6] 'Supposing, now, at this moment

[1] *Oed. Col.* 1586.   [2] In his lost *Polyxena.*   [3] § 2.
[4] Cf. Petronius, *Satyricon*, ch. i. *passim.*   [5] *Orest.* 264.
[6] *c. Timocrat.* 208.

a cry of alarm were heard outside the assize courts, and the news came that the prison was broken open and the prisoners escaped, is there any man here who is such a trifler that he would not run to the rescue at the top of his speed? But suppose someone came forward with the information that they had been set at liberty by the defendant, what then? Why, he would be lynched on the spot!' Compare also the way in which Hyperides excused himself, when he was proceeded against for bringing in a bill to liberate the slaves after Chaeronea. 'This measure', he said, 'was not drawn up by any orator, but by the battle of Chaeronea'. This striking image, being thrown in by the speaker in the midst of his proofs, enables him by one bold stroke to carry all mere logical objection before him. In all such cases our nature is drawn towards that which affects it most powerfully: hence an image lures us away from an argument: judgment is paralysed, matters of fact disappear from view, eclipsed by the superior blaze. Nor is it surprising that we should be thus affected; for when two forces are thus placed in juxtaposition, the stronger must always absorb into itself the weaker.

On sublimity of thought, and the manner in which it arises from native greatness of mind, from imitation, and from the employment of images, this brief outline must suffice.[1]

XVI

The subject which next claims our attention is that of figures of speech. I have already observed that figures, judiciously employed, play an important part in producing sublimity. It would be a tedious, or rather an endless task, to deal with every detail of this subject

[1] He passes over chs. x. xi.

here; so in order to establish what I have laid down, I will just run over, without further preface, a few of those figures which are most effective in lending grandeur to language.

Demosthenes is defending his policy; his natural line of argument would have been: 'You did not do wrong, men of Athens, to take upon yourselves the struggle for the liberties of Hellas. Of this you have home proofs. *They* did not wrong who fought at Marathon, at Salamis, and Plataea'. Instead of this, in a sudden moment of supreme exaltation he bursts out like some inspired prophet with that famous appeal to the mighty dead: 'Ye did not, could not have done wrong. I swear it by the men who faced the foe at Marathon!'[1] He employs the figure of adjuration, to which I will here give the name of Apostrophe. And what does he gain by it? He exalts the Athenian ancestors to the rank of divinities, showing that we ought to invoke those who have fallen for their country as gods; he fills the hearts of his judges with the heroic pride of the old warriors of Hellas; forsaking the beaten path of argument he rises to the loftiest altitude of grandeur and passion, and commands assent by the startling novelty of his appeal; he applies the healing charm of eloquence, and thus 'ministers to the mind diseased' of his countrymen, until lifted by his brave words above their misfortunes they begin to feel that the disaster of Chaeronea is no less glorious than the victories of Marathon and Salamis. All this he effects by the use of one figure, and so carries his hearers away with him. It is said that the germ of this adjuration is found in Eupolis:

'By mine own fight, by Marathon, I say,
    Who makes my heart to ache shall rue the day!'[2]

---

[1] *De Cor.* 208.   [2] In his (lost) *Demis.*

But there is nothing grand in the mere employment of an oath. Its grandeur will depend on its being employed in the right place and the right manner, on the right occasion, and with the right motive. In Eupolis the oath is nothing beyond an oath; and the Athenians to whom it is addressed are still prosperous, and in need of no consolation. Moreover, the poet does not, like Demosthenes, swear by the departed heroes as deities, so as to engender in his audience a just conception of their valour, but diverges from the champions to the battle—a mere lifeless thing. But Demosthenes has so skilfully managed the oath that in addressing his country-men after the defeat of Chaeronea he takes out of their minds all sense of disaster; and at the same time, while proving that no mistake has been made, he holds up an example, confirms his arguments by an oath, and makes his praise of the dead an incentive to the living. And to rebut a possible objection which occurred to him— 'Can you, Demosthenes, whose policy ended in defeat, swear by a victory?'—the orator proceeds to measure his language, choosing his very words so as to give no handle to opponents, thus showing us that even in our most inspired moments reason ought to hold the reins.[1] Let us mark his words: 'Those who *faced the foe* at Marathon; those who *fought in the sea-fights* of Salamis and Artemisium; those who *stood in the ranks* at Plataea.' Note that he nowhere says 'those who *conquered*,' art-fully suppressing any word which might hint at the successful issue of those battles, which would have spoilt the parallel with Chaeronea. And for the same reason he steals a march on his audience, adding immediately: 'All of whom, Aeschines—not those who were successful only—were buried by the state at the public expense'.

---

[1] Lit. 'That even in the midst of the revels of Bacchus we ought to remain sober'.

XVII

There is one truth which my studies have led me to observe, which perhaps it would be worth while to set down briefly here. It is this, that by a natural law the Sublime, besides receiving an acquisition of strength from figures, in its turn lends support in a remarkable manner to them. To explain: the use of figures has a peculiar tendency to rouse a suspicion of dishonesty, and to create an impression of treachery, scheming, and false reasoning; especially if the person addressed be a judge, who is master of the situation, and still more in the case of a despot, a king, a military potentate, or any of those who sit in high places.[1] If a man feels that this artful speaker is treating him like a silly boy and trying to throw dust in his eyes, he at once grows irritated, and thinking that such false reasoning implies a contempt of his understanding, he perhaps flies into a rage and will not hear another word; or even if he masters his resentment, still he is utterly indisposed to yield to the persuasive power of eloquence. Hence it follows that a figure is then most effectual when it appears in disguise. To allay, then, this distrust which attaches to the use of figures we must call in the powerful aid of sublimity and passion. For art, once associated with these great allies, will be overshadowed by their grandeur and beauty, and pass beyond the reach of all suspicion. To prove this I need only refer to the passage already quoted: 'I swear it by the men', etc. It is the very brilliancy of the orator's figure which blinds us to the fact that it *is* a figure. For as the fainter lustre of the stars is put out of sight by the all-encompassing rays of the sun, so when sublimity sheds its light all round the sophistries of rhetoric they become invisible. A similar

[1] Reading with Cobet, καὶ πάντας τοὺς ἐν ὑπεροχαῖς.

illusion is produced by the painter's art. When light and shadow are represented in colour, though they lie on the same surface side by side, it is the light which meets the eye first, and appears not only more conspicuous but also much nearer. In the same manner passion and grandeur of language, lying nearer to our souls by reason both of a certain natural affinity and of their radiance, always strike our mental eye before we become conscious of the figure, throwing its artificial character into the shade and hiding it as it were in a veil.

XVIII

The figures of question and interrogation also possess a specific quality which tends strongly to stir an audience and give energy to the speaker's words. 'Or tell me, do you want to run about asking one another, is there any news? what greater news could you have than that a man of Macedon is making himself master of Hellas? Is Philip dead? Not he. However, he is ill. But what is that to you? Even if anything happens to him you will soon raise up another Philip'.[1] Or this passage: 'Shall we sail against Macedon? And where, asks one, shall we effect a landing? The war itself will show us where Philip's weak places lie'.[1] Now if this had been put baldly it would have lost greatly in force. As we see it, it is full of the quick alternation of question and answer. The orator replies to himself as though he were meeting another man's objections. And this figure not only raises the tone of his words but makes them more convincing. For an exhibition of feeling has then most effect on an audience when it appears to flow naturally from the occasion, not to have been laboured by the

[1] *Phil.* i. 44.

art of the speaker; and this device of questioning and replying to himself reproduces the moment of passion. For as a sudden question addressed to an individual will sometimes startle him into a reply which is an unguarded expression of his genuine sentiments, so the figure of question and interrogation blinds the judgment of an audience, and deceives them into a belief that what is really the result of labour in every detail has been struck out of the speaker by the inspiration of the moment.

There is one passage in Herodotus which is generally credited with extraordinary sublimity. . . .

XIX

. . . The removal of connecting particles gives a quick rush and 'torrent rapture' to a passage, the writer appearing to be actually almost left behind by his own words. There is an example in Xenophon: 'Clashing their shields together they pushed, they fought, they slew, they fell'.[1] And the words of Eurylochus in the Odyssey:

'We passed at thy command the woodland's shade;
We found a stately hall built in a mountain glade'.[2]

Words thus severed from one another without the intervention of stops give a lively impression of one who through distress of mind at once halts and hurries in his speech. And this is what Homer has expressed by using the figure *Asyndeton*.

[1] Xen. *Hel.* iv. 3. 19.   [2] *Od.* x. 251.

XX

But nothing is so conducive to energy as a combination of different figures, when two or three uniting their resources mutually contribute to the vigour, the cogency, and the beauty of a speech. So Demosthenes in his speech against Meidias repeats the same words and breaks up his sentences in one lively descriptive passage: 'He who receives a blow is hurt in many ways which he could not even describe to another, by gesture, by look, by tone'. Then, to vary the movement of his speech, and prevent it from standing still (for stillness produces rest, but passion requires a certain disorder of language, imitating the agitation and commotion of the soul), he at once dashes off in another direction, breaking up his words again, and repeating them in a different form, 'by gesture, by look, by tone—when insult, when hatred, is added to violence, when he is struck with the fist, when he is struck as a slave!' By such means the orator imitates the action of Meidias, dealing blow upon blow on the minds of his judges. Immediately after like a hurricane he makes a fresh attack: 'When he is struck with the fist, when he is struck in the face; this is what moves, this is what maddens a man, unless he is inured to outrage; no one could describe all this so as to bring home to his hearers its bitterness'.[1] You see how he preserves, by continual variation, the intrinsic force of these repetitions and broken clauses, so that his order seems irregular, and conversely his irregularity acquires a certain measure of order.

[1] *Meid.* 72

XXI

Supposing we add the conjunctions, after the practice of Isocrates and his school: 'Moreover, I must not omit to mention that he who strikes a blow may hurt in many ways, in the first place by gesture, in the second place by look, in the third and last place by his tone'. If you compare the words thus set down in logical sequence with the expressions of the *Meidias*, you will see that the rapidity and rugged abruptness of passion, when all is made regular by connecting links, will be smoothed away, and the whole point and fire of the passage will at once disappear. For as, if you were to bind two runners together, they will forthwith be deprived of all liberty of movement, even so passion rebels against the trammels of conjunctions and other particles, because they curb its free rush and destroy the impression of mechanical impulse.

XXII

The figure hyperbaton belongs to the same class. By hyperbaton we mean a transposition of words or thoughts from their usual order, bearing unmistakably the characteristic stamp of violent mental agitation. In real life we often see a man under the influence of rage, or fear, or indignation, or beside himself with jealousy, or with some other out of the interminable list of human passions, begin a sentence, and then swerve aside into some inconsequent parenthesis, and then again double back to his original statement, being borne with quick turns by his distress, as though by a shifting wind, now this way, now that, and playing a thousand capricious variations on his words, his thoughts, and the natural order of his discourse. Now the figure hyperbaton is the means which is employed by the best writers to imitate these signs of natural emotion. For art is then perfect when it seems to be nature, and nature, again, is most effective when pervaded by the unseen presence of art. An illustration will be found in the speech of Dionysius of Phocaea in Herodotus: 'A hair's breadth now decides our destiny, Ionians, whether we shall live as freemen or as slaves—ay, as runaway slaves. Now, therefore, if you choose to endure a little hardship, you will be able at the cost of some present exertion to overcome your enemies'.[1] The regular sequence here would have been: 'Ionians, now is the time for you to endure a little hardship; for a hair's breadth will now decide our destiny'. But the Phocaean transposes the title 'Ionians', rushing at once to the subject of alarm, as though in the terror of the moment he had forgotten the usual address to his audience. Moreover, he inverts the logical order of his thoughts, and instead of beginning with the necessity for exertion, which is the point he wishes to urge upon them, he first gives them the reason for that necessity in the words, 'a hair's breadth now decides our destiny', so that his words seem unpremeditated, and forced upon him by the crisis.

Thucydides surpasses all other writers in the bold use of this figure, even breaking up sentences which are by their nature absolutely one and indivisible. But nowhere do we find it so unsparingly employed as in Demosthenes, who though not so daring in his manner of using it as the elder writer is very happy in giving to his speeches by frequent transpositions the lively air of unstudied debate. Moreover, he drags, as it were, his

[1] vi. 11.

audience with him into the perils of a long inverted clause. He often begins to say something, then leaves the thought in suspense, meanwhile thrusting in between, in a position apparently foreign and unnatural, some extraneous matters, one upon another, and having thus made his hearers fear lest the whole discourse should break down, and forced them into eager sympathy with the danger of the speaker, when he is nearly at the end of a period he adds just at the right moment, i.e. when it is least expected, the point which they have been waiting for so long. And thus by the very boldness and hazard of his inversions he produces a much more astounding effect. I forbear to cite examples, as they are too numerous to require it.

XXIII

The juxtaposition of different cases, the enumeration of particulars, and the use of contrast and climax, all, as you know, add much vigour, and give beauty and great elevation and life to a style. The diction also gains greatly in diversity and movement by changes of case, time, person, number, and gender.

With regard to change of number: not only is the style improved by the use of those words which, though singular in form, are found on inspection to be plural in meaning, as in the lines:

'A countless host dispersed along the sand
   With joyous cries the shoal of tunny hailed',

but it is more worthy of observation that plurals for singulars sometimes fall with a more impressive dignity, rousing the imagination by the mere sense of vast

number. Such is the effect of those words of Oedipus
in Sophocles:

> 'Oh fatal, fatal ties!
> Ye gave us birth, and we being born ye sowed
> The self-same seed, and gave the world to view
> Sons, brothers, sires, domestic murder foul,
> Brides, mothers, wives. . . . Ay, ye laid bare
> The blackest, deepest place where Shame can dwell'.[1]

Here we have in either case but one person, first Oedipus,
then Jocasta; but the expansion of number into the
plural gives an impression of multiplied calamity. So
in the following plurals:

> 'There came forth Hectors, and there came Sarpedons'.

And in those words of Plato's (which we have already
adduced elsewhere), referring to the Athenians: 'We have
no Pelopses or Cadmuses or Aegyptuses or Danauses,
or any others out of all the mob of Hellenized barbarians,
dwelling among us; no, this is the land of pure Greeks,
with no mixture of foreign elements',[2] etc. Such an
accumulation of words in the plural number necessarily
gives greater pomp and sound to a subject. But we
must only have recourse to this device when the nature
of our theme makes it allowable to amplify, to multiply,
or to speak in the tones of exaggeration or passion. To
overlay every sentence with ornament [3] is very pedantic.

XXIV

On the other hand, the contraction of plurals into
singulars sometimes creates an appearance of great

---

[1] *O. R.* 1403.   [2] *Menex.* 245, D.
[3] Lit. 'To hang bells everywhere', a metaphor from the bells
which were attached to horses' trappings on festive occasions.

dignity; as in that phrase of Demosthenes: 'Thereupon all Peloponnesus was divided'.[1]   There is another in Herodotus: 'When Phrynichus brought a drama on the stage entitled *The Taking of Miletus*, the whole theatre fell a weeping'—instead of 'all the spectators'.   This knitting together of a number of scattered particulars into one whole gives them an aspect of corporate life.   And the beauty of both uses lies, I think, in their betokening emotion, by giving a sudden change of complexion to the circumstances—whether a word which is strictly singular is unexpectedly changed into a plural—or whether a number of isolated units are combined by the use of a single sonorous word under one head.

XXV

When past events are introduced as happening in present time the narrative form is changed into a dramatic action.   Such is that description in Xenophon: 'A man who has fallen and is being trampled under foot by Cyrus's horse, strikes the belly of the animal with his scimitar; the horse starts aside and unseats Cyrus, and he falls'.   Similarly in many passages of Thucydides.

XXVI

Equally dramatic is the interchange of persons, often making a reader fancy himself to be moving in the midst of the perils described:

'Unwearied, thou wouldst deem, with toil unspent,
    They met in war; so furiously they fought'.[2]

[1] *De Cor.* 18.   [2] *Il.* xv. 697.

and that line in Aratus:

　'Beware that month to tempt the surging sea'.[1]

In the same way Herodotus: 'Passing from the city of Elephantine you will sail upwards until you reach a level plain. You cross this region, and there entering another ship you will sail on for two days, and so reach a great city, whose name is Meroe'.[2] Observe how he takes us, as it were, by the hand, and leads us in spirit through these places, making us no longer readers, but spectators. Such a direct personal address always has the effect of placing the reader in the midst of the scene of action. And by pointing your words to the individual reader, instead of to the readers generally, as in the line

　'Thou had'st not known for whom Tydides fought',[3]

and thus exciting him by an appeal to himself, you will rouse interest, and fix attention, and make him a partaker in the action of the book.

XXVII

　Sometimes, again, a writer in the midst of a narrative in the third person suddenly steps aside and makes a transition to the first. It is a kind of figure which strikes like a sudden outburst of passion. Thus Hector in the Iliad:

　'With mighty voice called to the men of Troy
　To storm the ships, and leave the bloody spoils:
　If any I behold with willing foot
　Shunning the ships, and lingering on the plain,
　That hour I will contrive his death'.[4]

The poet then takes upon himself the narrative part, as being his proper business; but this abrupt threat he

[1] *Phaen.* 287.　　[2] ii. 29.　　[3] *Il.* v. 85.　　[4] *Il.* xv. 346.

attributes, without a word of warning, to the enraged
Trojan chief. To have interposed any such words as
'Hector said so and so' would have had a frigid effect.
As the lines stand the writer is left behind by his own
words, and the transition is effected while he is preparing
for it. Accordingly the proper use of this figure is in
dealing with some urgent crisis which will not allow the
writer to linger, but compels him to make a rapid change
from one person to another. So in Hecataeus: 'Now
Ceyx took this in dudgeon, and straightway bade the
children of Heracles to depart. "Behold, I can give you
no help; lest, therefore, ye perish yourselves and bring
hurt upon me also, get ye forth into some other land"'.
There is a different use of the change of persons in the
speech of Demosthenes against Aristogeiton, which places
before us the quick turns of violent emotion. 'Is there
none to be found among you', he asks, 'who even feels
indignation at the outrageous conduct of a loathsome
and shameless wretch who—vilest of men, when you
were debarred from freedom of speech, not by barriers
or by doors, which might indeed be opened',[1] etc. Thus
in the midst of a half-expressed thought he makes a
quick change of front, and having almost in his anger
torn one word into two persons, 'who, vilest of men',
etc., he then breaks off his address to Aristogeiton, and
seems to leave him, nevertheless, by the passion of his
utterance, rousing all the more the attention of the
court. The same feature may be observed in a speech
of Penelope's:

'Why com'st thou, Medon, from the wooers proud?
Com'st thou to bid the handmaids of my lord
To cease their tasks, and make for them good cheer?
Ill fare their wooing, and their gathering here!

[1] *c. Aristog.* i. 27.

Would God that here this hour they all might take
Their last, their latest meal! Who day by day
Make here your muster, to devour and waste
The substance of my son: have ye not heard
When children at your fathers' knee the deeds
And prowess of your king?'[1]

XXVIII

None, I suppose, would dispute the fact that periphrasis tends much to sublimity. For, as in music the
simple air is rendered more pleasing by the addition of
harmony, so in language periphrasis often sounds in
concord with a literal expression, adding much to the
beauty of its tone—provided always that it is not
inflated and harsh, but agreeably blended. To confirm
this one passage from Plato will suffice—the opening
words of his Funeral Oration: 'In deed these men have
now received from us their due, and that tribute paid
they are now passing on their destined journey, with the
State speeding them all and his own friends speeding
each one of them on his way'.[2] Death, you see, he calls
the 'destined journey'; to receive the rites of burial is
to be publicly 'sped on your way' by the State. And
these turns of language lend dignity in no common
measure to the thought. He takes the words in their
naked simplicity and handles them as a musician, investing them with melody—harmonizing them, as it
were—by the use of periphrasis. So Xenophon:
'Labour you regard as the guide to a pleasant life, and
you have laid up in your souls the fairest and most
soldier-like of all gifts: in praise is your delight, more
than in anything else'.[3] By saying, instead of 'you are

[1] *Od.* iv. 681.   [2] *Menex*, 236, D.   [3] *Cyrop.* i. 5. 12.

ready to labour', 'you regard labour as the guide to a pleasant life', and by similarly expanding the rest of that passage, he gives to his eulogy a much wider and loftier range of sentiment.   Let us add that inimitable phrase in Herodotus: 'Those Scythians who pillaged the temple were smitten from heaven by a female malady'.

XXIX

But this figure, more than any other, is very liable to abuse, and great restraint is required in employing it. It soon begins to carry an impression of feebleness, savours of vapid trifling, and arouses disgust.   Hence Plato, who is very bold and not always happy in his use of figures, is much ridiculed for saying in his *Laws* that 'neither gold nor silver wealth must be allowed to establish itself in our State',[1] suggesting, it is said, that if he had forbidden property in oxen or sheep he would certainly have spoken of it as 'bovine and ovine wealth'.

Here we must quit this part of our subject, hoping, my dear friend Terentian, that your learned curiosity will be satisfied with this short excursion on the use of figures in their relation to the Sublime.   All those which I have mentioned help to render a style more energetic and impassioned; and passion contributes as largely to sublimity as the delineation of character to amusement.

XXX

But since the thoughts conveyed by words and the expression of those thoughts are for the most part

[1] *De Legg.* vii. 801, B.

interwoven with one another, we will now add some considerations which have hitherto been overlooked on the subject of expression. To say that the choice of appropriate and striking words has a marvellous power and an enthralling charm for the reader, that this is the main object of pursuit with all orators and writers, that it is this, and this alone, which causes the works of literature to exhibit the glowing perfections of the finest statues, their grandeur, their beauty, their mellowness, their dignity, their energy, their power, and all their other graces, and that it is this which endows the facts with a vocal soul; to say all this would, I fear, be, to the initiated, an impertinence. Indeed, we may say with strict truth that beautiful words are the very light of thought. I do not mean to say that imposing language is appropriate to every occasion. A trifling subject tricked out in grand and stately words would have the same effect as a huge tragic mask placed on the head of a little child. Only in poetry and . . .

XXXI

. . . There is a genuine ring in that line of Anacreon's:

'The Thracian filly I no longer heed'.

The same merit belongs to that original phrase in Theophrastus; to me, at least, from the closeness of its analogy, it seems to have a peculiar expressiveness, though Caecilius censures it, without telling us why. 'Philip', says the historian, 'showed a marvellous alacrity in *taking doses of trouble*'. We see from this that the most homely language is sometimes far more vivid than the most ornamental, being recognized at once as the language of common life, and gaining immediate currency by its familiarity. In speaking, then, of Philip as 'taking doses of trouble', Theopompus has laid hold on a phrase which describes with peculiar vividness one who for the sake of advantage endured what was base and sordid with patience and cheerfulness. The same may be observed of two passages in Herodotus: 'Cleomenes having lost his wits, cut his own flesh into pieces with a short sword, until by gradually *mincing* his whole body he destroyed himself';[1] and 'Pythes continued fighting on his ship until he was entirely *hacked to pieces*'.[2] Such terms come home at once to the vulgar reader, but their own vulgarity is redeemed by their expressiveness.

XXXII

Concerning the number of metaphors to be employed together Caecilius seems to give his vote with those critics who make a law that not more than two, or at the utmost three, should be combined in the same place. The use, however, must be determined by the occasion. Those outbursts of passion which drive onwards like a winter torrent draw with them as an indispensable accessory whole masses of metaphor. It is thus in that passage of Demosthenes (who here also is our safest guide): 'Those vile fawning wretches, each one of whom has lopped from his country her fairest members, who have toasted away their liberty, first to Philip, now to Alexander, who measure happiness by their belly and their vilest appetites, who have overthrown the old landmarks and standards of felicity among Greeks—to be freemen, and to have no one for a master.'[3] Here the number of the metaphors is obscured by the orator's indignation against the betrayers of his country. And

[1] vi. 75.　　[2] vii. 181.　　[3] *De Cor.* 296.

to effect this Aristotle and Theophrastus recommend the softening of harsh metaphors by the use of some such phrase as 'So to say', 'As it were', 'If I may be permitted the expression', 'If so bold a term is allowable'. For thus to forestall criticism[1] mitigates, they assert, the boldness of the metaphors. And I will not deny that these have their use. Nevertheless I must repeat the remark which I made in the case of figures,[2] and maintain that there are native antidotes to the number and boldness of metaphors, in well-timed displays of strong feeling, and in unaffected sublimity, because these have an innate power by the dash of their movement of sweeping along and carrying all else before them. Or should we not rather say that they absolutely demand as indispensable the use of daring metaphors, and will not allow the hearer to pause and criticize the number of them, because he shares the passion of the speaker?

In the treatment, again, of familiar topics and in descriptive passages nothing gives such distinctness as a close and continuous series of metaphors. It is by this means that Xenophon has so finely delineated the anatomy of the human frame.[3] And there is a still more brilliant and lifelike picture in Plato.[4] The human head he calls a *citadel*; the neck is an *isthmus* set to divide it from the chest; to support it beneath are the vertebrae, turning like *hinges*; pleasure he describes as a *bait* to tempt men to ill; the tongue is the *arbiter of tastes*. The heart is at once the *knot* of the veins and the *source* of the rapidly circulating blood, and is stationed in the *guard-room* of the body. The ramifying blood-vessels he calls *alleys*. 'And casting about', he says, 'for something to sustain the violent palpitation of the heart when

---

[1] Reading ὑποτίμησις.   [2] Ch. xvii.   [3] *Memorab.* i. 4, 5.
[4] *Timaeus*, 69, D; 74, A; 65, C; 72, G; 74, B, D; 80, E; 77, G; 78, E; 85, E.

it is alarmed by the approach of danger or agitated by passion, since at such times it is overheated, they (the gods) implanted in us the lungs, which are so fashioned that being soft and bloodless, and having cavities within, they act like a buffer, and when the heart boils with inward passion by yielding to its throbbing save it from injury'. He compares the seat of the desires to the *women's quarters*, the seat of the passions to the *men's quarters*, in a house. The spleen, again, is the *napkin* of the internal organs, by whose excretions it is saturated from time to time, and swells to a great size with inward impurity. 'After this', he continues, 'they shrouded the whole with flesh, throwing it forward, like a cushion, as a barrier against injuries from without'. The blood he terms the *pasture* of the flesh. 'To assist the process of nutrition', he goes on, 'they divided the body into ducts, cutting trenches like those in a garden, so that, the body being a system of narrow conduits, the current of the veins might flow as from a perennial fountain-head. And when the end is at hand', he says, 'the soul is cast loose from her moorings like a ship, and free to wander whither she will'. These, and a hundred similar fancies, follow one another in quick succession. But those which I have pointed out are sufficient to demonstrate how great is the natural power of figurative language, and how largely metaphors conduce to sublimity, and to illustrate the important part which they play in all impassioned and descriptive passages.

That the use of figurative language, as of all other beauties of style, has a constant tendency towards excess, is an obvious truth which I need not dwell upon. It is chiefly on this account that even Plato comes in for a large share of disparagement, because he is often carried away by a sort of frenzy of language into an intemperate use of violent metaphors and inflated allegory. 'It is not easy to remark' (he says in one place) 'that a city ought to be blended like a bowl, in which the mad wine boils when it is poured out, but being disciplined by another and a sober god in that fair society produces a good and temperate drink.[1] Really, it is said, to speak of water as a 'sober god', and of the process of mixing as a 'discipline', is to talk like a poet, and no very *sober* one either. It was such defects as these that the hostile critic [2] Caecilius made his ground of attack, when he had the boldness in his essay 'On the Beauties of Lysias' to pronounce that writer superior in every respect to Plato. Now Caecilius was doubly unqualified for a judge: he loved Lysias better even than himself, and at the same time his hatred of Plato and all his works is greater even than his love for Lysias. Moreover, he is so blind a partisan that his very premises are open to dispute. He vaunts Lysias as a faultless and immaculate writer, while Plato is, according to him, full of blemishes. Now this is not the case: far from it.

XXXIII

But supposing now that we assume the existence of a really unblemished and irreproachable writer. Is it not worth while to raise the whole question whether in poetry and prose we should prefer sublimity accompanied by some faults, or a style which never rising above moderate excellence never stumbles and never requires correction? and again, whether the first place in literature is justly to be assigned to the more numerous, or the loftier excellences? For these are questions proper to

[1] *Legg.* vi. 773, G.
[2] Reading ὁ μισῶν αὐτόν, by a conjecture of the translator.

an inquiry on the Sublime, and urgently asking for settlement.

I know, then, that the largest intellects are far from being the most exact. A mind always intent on correctness is apt to be dissipated in trifles; but in great affluence of thought, as in vast material wealth, there must needs be an occasional neglect of detail. And is it not inevitably so? Is it not by risking nothing, by never aiming high, that a writer of low or middling powers keeps generally clear of faults and secure of blame? whereas the loftier walks of literature are by their very loftiness perilous? I am well aware, again, that there is a law by which in all human productions the weak points catch the eye first, by which their faults remain indelibly stamped on the memory, while their beauties quickly fade away. Yet, though I have myself noted not a few faulty passages in Homer and in other authors of the highest rank, and though I am far from being partial to their failings, nevertheless I would call them not so much wilful blunders as oversights which were allowed to pass unregarded through that contempt of little things, that 'brave disorder', which is natural to an exalted genius; and I still think that the greater excellences, though not everywhere equally sustained, ought always to be voted to the first place in literature, if for no other reason, for the mere grandeur of soul they evince. Let us take an instance: Apollonius in his *Argonautica* has given us a poem actually faultless; and in his pastoral poetry Theocritus is eminently happy, except when he occasionally attempts another style. And what then? Would you rather be a Homer or an Apollonius? Or take Eratosthenes and his *Erigone*; because that little work is without a flaw, is he therefore a greater poet than Archilochus, with all his disorderly profusion? greater than that impetuous, that god-gifted genius, which chafed against the restraints of law? or in lyric poetry would you choose to be a Bacchylides or a Pindar? in tragedy a Sophocles or (save the mark!) an Io of Chios? Yet Io and Bacchylides never stumble, their style is always neat, always pretty; while Pindar and Sophocles sometimes move onwards with a wide blaze of splendour, but often drop out of view in sudden and disastrous eclipse. Nevertheless no one in his senses would deny that a single play of Sophocles, the *Oedipus*, is of higher value than all the dramas of Io put together.

XXXIV

If the number and not the loftiness of an author's merits is to be our standard of success, judged by this test we must admit that Hyperides is a far superior orator to Demosthenes. For in Hyperides there is a richer modulation, a greater variety of excellence. He is, we may say, in everything second-best, like the champion of the *pentathlon*, who, though in every contest he has to yield the prize to some other combatant, is superior to the unpractised in all five. Not only has he rivalled the success of Demosthenes in everything but his manner of composition, but, as though that were not enough, he has taken in all the excellences and graces of Lysias as well. He knows when it is proper to speak with simplicity, and does not, like Demosthenes, continue the same key throughout. His touches of character are racy and sparkling, and full of a delicate flavour. Then how admirable is his wit, how polished his raillery! How well bred he is, how dexterous in the use of irony! His jests are pointed, but without any of the grossness and vulgarity of the old Attic comedy. He is skilled in making light of an opponent's argument, full of a well-aimed satire which amuses while it stings; and through all this there runs a pervading, may we not say, a matchless charm. He is most apt in moving compassion; his mythical digressions show a fluent ease, and he is perfect in bending his course and finding a way out of them without violence or effort. Thus when he tells the story of Leto he is really almost a poet; and his funeral oration shows a declamatory magnificence to which I hardly know a parallel. Demosthenes, on the other hand, has no touches of character, none of the versatility, fluency, or declamatory skill of Hyperides. He is, in fact, almost entirely destitute of all those excellences which I have just enumerated. When he makes violent efforts to be humorous and witty, the only laughter he arouses is against himself; and the nearer he tries to get to the winning grace of Hyperides, the farther he recedes from it. Had he, for instance, attempted such a task as the little speech in defence of Phryne or Athenagoras, he would only have added to the reputation of his rival. Nevertheless all the beauties of Hyperides, however numerous, cannot make him sublime. He never exhibits strong feeling, has little energy, rouses no emotion; certainly he never kindles terror in the breast of his readers. But Demosthenes followed a great master,[1] and drew his consummate excellences, his high-pitched eloquence, his living passion, his copiousness, his sagacity, his speed—that mastery and power which can never be approached—from the highest of sources. These mighty, these heaven-sent gifts (I dare not call them human), he made his own both one and all. Therefore, I say, by the noble qualities which he does possess he remains supreme above all rivals, and throws a cloud over his failings, silencing by his thunders and

---

[1] i.e. Thucydides.

blinding by his lightnings the orators of all ages. Yes, it would be easier to meet the lightning-stroke with steady eye than to gaze unmoved when his impassioned eloquence is sending out flash after flash.

.

XXXV

But in the case of Plato and Lysias there is, as I said, a further difference. Not only is Lysias vastly inferior to Plato in the degree of his merits, but in their number as well; and at the same time he is as far ahead of Plato in the number of his faults as he is behind in that of his merits.

What truth, then, was it that was present to those mighty spirits of the past, who, making whatever is greatest in writing their aim, thought it beneath them to be exact in every detail? Among many others especially this, that it was not in nature's plan for us her chosen children to be creatures base and ignoble —no, she brought us into life, and into the whole universe, as into some great field of contest, that we should be at once spectators and ambitious rivals of her mighty deeds, and from the first implanted in our souls an invincible yearning for all that is great, all that is diviner than ourselves. Therefore even the whole world is not wide enough for the soaring range of human thought, but man's mind often overleaps the very bounds of space.[1] When we survey the whole circle of life, and see it abounding everywhere in what is elegant, grand, and beautiful, we learn at once what is the true end of man's being. And this is why nature prompts us to admire, not the clearness and usefulness of a little stream, but

[1] Cf. Lucretius on Epicurus: 'Ergo vivida vis animi pervicit, et extra Processit longe flammantia moenia mundi,' etc.

the Nile, the Danube, the Rhine, and far beyond all the Ocean; not to turn our wandering eyes from the heavenly fires, though often darkened, to the little flame kindled by human hands, however pure and steady its light; not to think that tiny lamp more wondrous than the caverns of Aetna, from whose raging depths are hurled up stones and whole masses of rock, and torrents sometimes come pouring from earth's centre of pure and living fire.

To sum the whole: whatever is useful or needful lies easily within man's reach; but he keeps his homage for what is astounding.

XXXVI

How much more do these principles apply to the Sublime in literature, where grandeur is never, as it sometimes is in nature, dissociated from utility and advantage. Therefore all those who have achieved it, however far from faultless, are still more than mortal. When a writer uses any other resource he shows himself to be a man; but the Sublime lifts him near to the great spirit of the Deity. He who makes no slips must be satisfied with negative approbation, but he who is sublime commands positive reverence. Why need I add that each one of those great writers often redeems all his errors by one grand and masterly stroke? But the strongest point of all is that, if you were to pick out all the blunders of Homer, Demosthenes, Plato, and all the greatest names in literature, and add them together, they would be found to bear a very small, or rather an infinitesimal proportion to the passages in which these supreme masters have attained absolute perfection. Therefore it is that all posterity, whose judgment envy herself cannot impeach, has brought and bestowed on them the crown of glory, has guarded their fame until this day against all attack, and is likely to preserve it

> 'As long as lofty trees shall grow,
> And restless waters seaward flow'.

It has been urged by one writer that we should not prefer the huge disproportioned Colossus to the Doryphorus of Polycletus. But (to give one out of many possible answers) in art we admire exactness, in the works of nature magnificence; and it is from nature that man derives the faculty of speech. Whereas, then, in statuary we look for close resemblance to humanity, in literature we require something which transcends humanity. Nevertheless (to reiterate the advice which we gave at the beginning of this essay), since that success which consists in avoidance of error is usually the gift of art, while high, though unequal excellence is the attribute of genius, it is proper on all occasions to call in art as an ally to nature. By the combined resources of these two we may hope to achieve perfection.

Such are the conclusions which were forced upon me concerning the points at issue; but every one may consult his own taste.

XXXVII

To return, however, from this long digression; closely allied to metaphors are comparisons and similes, differing only in this   *   *   *[1]

[1] The asterisks denote gaps in the original text.

XXXVIII

Such absurdities as: 'Unless you carry your brains next to the ground in your heels'.[1]   Hence it is necessary to know where to draw the line; for if ever it is overstepped the effect of the hyperbole is spoilt, being in such cases relaxed by overstraining, and producing the very opposite to the effect desired. Isocrates, for instance, from an ambitious desire of lending everything a strong rhetorical colouring, shows himself in quite a childish light.   Having in his Panegyrical Oration set himself to prove that the Athenian state has surpassed that of Sparta in her services to Hellas, he starts off at the very outset with these words: 'Such is the power of language that it can extenuate what is great, and lend greatness to what is little, give freshness to what is antiquated, and describe what is recent so that it seems to be of the past'.[2]   Come, Isocrates (it might be asked), is it thus that you are going to tamper with the facts about Sparta and Athens?   This flourish about the power of language is like a signal hung out to warn his audience not to believe him.   We may repeat here what we said about figures, and say that the hyperbole is then most effective when it appears in disguise.   And this effect is produced when a writer, impelled by strong feeling, speaks in the accent of some tremendous crisis; as Thucydides does in describing the massacre in Sicily. 'The Syracusans,' he says, 'went down after them, and slew those especially who were in the river, and the water was at once defiled, yet still they went on drinking it, though mingled with mud and gore, most of them even fighting for it'.[3]   The drinking of mud and gore,

[1] Pseud. Dem. de Halon. 45.   [2] Paneg. 8.
[3] Thuc. vii. 84.

and even the fighting for it, is made credible by the awful horror of the scene described. Similarly Herodotus on those who fell at Thermopylae: 'Here as they fought, those who still had them, with daggers, the rest with hands and teeth, the barbarians buried them under their javelins'.[1] That they fought with the teeth against heavy-armed assailants, and that they were buried with javelins, are perhaps hard sayings, but not incredible, for the reasons already explained. We can see that these circumstances have not been dragged in to produce a hyperbole, but that the hyperbole has grown naturally out of the circumstances. For, as I am never tired of explaining, in actions and passions verging on frenzy there lies a kind of remission and palliation of any licence of language. Hence some comic extravagances, however improbable, gain credence by their humour, such as:

'He had a farm, a little farm, where space severely
    pinches;
'Twas smaller than the last dispatch from Sparta by
    some inches'.

For mirth is one of the passions, having its seat in pleasure. And hyperboles may be employed either to increase or to lessen—since exaggeration is common to both uses. Thus in extenuating an opponent's argument we try to make it seem smaller than it is.

XXXIX

We have still left, my dear sir, the fifth of those sources which we set down at the outset as contributing

[1] vii. 225.

to sublimity, that which consists in the mere arrangement of words in a certain order. Having already published two books dealing fully with this subject—so far at least as our investigations had carried us—it will be sufficient for the purpose of our present inquiry to add that harmony is an instrument which has a natural power, not only to win and to delight, but also in a remarkable degree to exalt the soul and sway the heart of man. When we see that a flute kindles certain emotions in its hearers, rendering them almost beside themselves and full of an orgiastic frenzy, and that by starting some kind of rhythmical beat it compels him who listens to move in time and assimilate his gestures to the tune, even though he has no taste whatever for music; when we know that the sounds of a harp, which in themselves have no meaning, by the change of key, by the mutual relation of the notes, and their arrangement in symphony, often lay a wonderful spell on an audience—though these are mere shadows and spurious imitations of persuasion, not, as I have said, genuine manifestations of human nature—can we doubt that composition (being a kind of harmony of that language which nature has taught us, and which reaches, not our ears only, but our very souls), when it raises changing forms of words, of thoughts, of actions, of beauty, of melody, all of which are engrained in and akin to ourselves, and when by the blending of its manifold tones it brings home to the minds of those who stand by the feelings present to the speaker, and ever disposes the hearer to sympathize with those feelings, adding word to word, until it has raised a majestic and harmonious structure—can we wonder if all this enchants us, wherever we meet with it, and filling us with the sense of pomp and dignity and sublimity, and whatever else it enbraces, gains a complete mastery over our minds?

It would be mere infatuation to join issue on truths so universally acknowledged, and established by experience beyond dispute.[1]

Now to give an instance: that is doubtless a sublime thought, indeed wonderfully fine, which Demosthenes applies to his decree: τοῦτο τὸ ψήφισμα τὸν τότε τῇ πόλει περιστάντα κίνδυνον παρελθεῖν ἐποίησεν ὥσπερ νέφος, 'This decree caused the danger which then hung round our city to pass away like a cloud'. But the modulation is as perfect as the sentiment itself is weighty. It is uttered wholly in the dactylic measure, the noblest and most magnificent of all measures, and hence forming the chief constituent in the finest metre we know, the heroic. [And it is with great judgment that the words ὥσπερ νέφος are reserved till the end.[2]] Supposing we transpose them from their proper place and read, say: τοῦτο τὸ ψήφισμα ὥσπερ νέφος ἐποίησε τὸν τότε κίνδυνον παρελθεῖν—nay, let us merely cut off one syllable, reading ἐποίησε παρελθεῖν ὡς νέφος—and you will understand how close is the unison between harmony and sublimity. In the passage before us the words ὥσπερ νέφος move first in a heavy measure, which is metrically equivalent to four short syllables: but on removing one syllable, and reading ὡς νέφος, the grandeur of movement is at once crippled by the abridgment. So conversely if you lengthen into ὡσπερεὶ νέφος, the meaning is still the same, but it does not strike the ear in the same manner, because by lingering over the final syllables you at once dissipate and relax the abrupt grandeur of the passage.

[1] Reading ἀλλ' ἔοικε μανία, and putting a full stop at πίστις.
[2] There is a break here in the text; but the context indicates the sense of the words lost, which has accordingly been supplied.

XL

There is another method very efficient in exalting a style. As the different members of the body, none of which, if severed from its connection, has any intrinsic excellence, unite by their mutual combination to form a complete and perfect organism, so also the elements of a fine passage, by whose separation from one another its high quality is simultaneously dissipated and evaporates, when joined in one organic whole, and still further compacted by the bond of harmony, by the mere rounding of the period gain power of tone. In fact, a clause may be said to derive its sublimity from the joint contributions of a number of particulars. And further (as we have shown at large elsewhere), many writers in prose and verse, though their natural powers were not high, were perhaps even low, and though the terms they employed were usually common and popular and conveying no impression of refinement, by the mere harmony of their composition have attained dignity and elevation, and avoided the appearance of meanness. Such among many others are Philistus, Aristophanes occasionally, Euripides almost always. Thus when Heracles says, after the murder of his children:

'I'm full of woes, I have no room for more',[1]

the words are quite common, but they are made sublime by being cast in a fine mould. By changing their position you will see that the poetical quality of Euripides depends more on his arrangement than on his thoughts. Compare his lines on Dirce dragged by the bull:

'Whatever crossed his path,
Caught in his victim's form, he seized, and dragging
Oak, woman, rock, now here, now there, he flies'.[2]

[1] *H. F.* 1245.   [2] *Antiope* (Nauck, 222).

The circumstance is noble in itself, but it gains in vigour because the language is disposed so as not to hurry the movement, not running, as it were, on wheels, because there is a distinct stress on each word, and the time is delayed, advancing slowly to a pitch of stately sublimity.

XLI

Nothing so much degrades the tone of a style as an effeminate and hurried movement in the language, such as is produced by pyrrhics and trochees and dichorees falling in time together into a regular dance measure. Such abuse of rhythm is sure to savour of coxcombry and petty affectation, and grows tiresome in the highest degree by a monotonous sameness of tone. But its worst effect is that, as those who listen to a ballad have their attention distracted from its subject and can think of nothing but the tune, so an over-rhythmical passage does not affect the hearer by the meaning of its words, but merely by their cadence, so that sometimes, knowing where the pause must come, they beat time with the speaker, striking the expected close like dancers before the stop is reached. Equally undignified is the splitting up of a sentence into a number of little words and short syllables crowded too closely together and forced into cohesion—hammered, as it were, successively together —after the manner of mortice and tenon.[1]

[1] I must refer to Weiske's Note, which I have followed, for the probable interpretation of this extraordinary passage.

XLII

Sublimity is further diminished by cramping the diction. Deformity instead of grandeur ensues from over-compression. Here I am not referring to a judicious compactness of phrase, but to a style which is dwarfed, and its force frittered away To cut your words too short is to prune away their sense, but to be concise is to be direct. On the other hand, we know that a style becomes lifeless by over-extension, I mean by being relaxed to an unseasonable length.

XLIII

The use of mean words has also a strong tendency to degrade a lofty passage. Thus in that description of the storm in Herodotus the matter is admirable, but some of the words admitted are beneath the dignity of the subject; such, perhaps, as 'the seas having *seethed*', because the ill-sounding phrase 'having seethed' detracts much from its impressiveness: or when he says 'the wind wore away', and 'those who clung round the wreck met with an unwelcome end'.[1] 'Wore away' is ignoble and vulgar, and 'unwelcome' inadequate to the extent of the disaster.

Similarly Theopompus, after giving a fine picture of the Persian king's descent against Egypt, has exposed the whole to censure by certain paltry expressions. 'There was no city, no people of Asia, which did not send an embassy to the king; no product of the earth, no work of art, whether beautiful or precious, which was not among the gifts brought to him. Many and costly

[1] vii. 188, 191, 13.

were the hangings and robes, some purple, some embroidered, some white; many the tents, of cloth of gold,
furnished with all things useful; many the tapestries and
couches of great price. Moreover, there was gold and
silver plate richly wrought, goblets and bowls, some of
which might be seen studded with gems, and others
besides worked in relief with great skill and at vast
expense. Besides these there were suits of armour in
number past computation, partly Greek, partly foreign,
endless trains of baggage animals and fat cattle for
slaughter, many bushels of spices, many panniers and
sacks and sheets of writing-paper; and all other neces-
saries in the same proportion. And there was salt meat
of all kinds of beasts in immense quantity, heaped
together to such a height as to show at a distance like
mounds and hills thrown up one against another'. He
runs off from the grander parts of his subject to the
meaner, and sinks where he ought to rise. Still worse,
by his mixing up *panniers* and *spices* and *bags* with his
wonderful recital of that vast and busy scene one would
imagine that he was describing a kitchen. Let us suppose that in that show of magnificence someone had
taken a set of wretched baskets and bags and placed
them in the midst, among vessels of gold, jewelled bowls,
silver plate, and tents and goblets of gold; how incongruous would have seemed the effect! Now just in the
same way these petty words, introduced out of season,
stand out like deformities and blots on the diction.
These details might have been given in one or two broad
strokes, as when he speaks of mounds being heaped
together. So in dealing with the other preparations he
might have told us of 'wagons and camels and a long
train of baggage animals loaded with all kinds of supplies
for the luxury and enjoyment of the table', or have
mentioned 'piles of grain of every species, and of all the

choicest delicacies required by the art of the cook or the taste of the epicure', or (if he must needs be so very precise) he might have spoken of 'whatever dainties are supplied by those who lay or those who dress the banquet'. In our sublimer efforts we should never stoop to what is sordid and despicable, unless very hard pressed by some urgent necessity. If we would write becomingly, our utterance should be worthy of our theme. We should take a lesson from nature, who when she planned the human frame did not set our grosser parts, or the ducts for purging the body, in our face, but as far as she could concealed them, 'diverting', as Xenophon says, 'those canals as far as possible from our senses',[1] and thus shunning in any part to mar the beauty of the whole creature.

However, it is not incumbent on us to specify and enumerate whatever diminishes a style. We have now pointed out the various means of giving it nobility and loftiness. It is clear, then, that whatever is contrary to these will generally degrade and deform it.

XLIV

There is still another point which remains to be cleared up, my dear Terentian, and on which I shall not hesitate to add some remarks, to gratify your inquiring spirit. It relates to a question which was recently put to me by a certain philosopher. 'To me', he said, 'in common, I may say, with many others, it is a matter of wonder that in the present age, which produces many highly skilled in the arts of popular persuasion, many of keen and active powers, many especially rich in every pleasing

[1] *Mem.* i. 4. 6.

gift of language, the growth of highly exalted and wide-reaching genius has with a few rare exceptions almost entirely ceased. So universal is the dearth of eloquence which prevails throughout the world. Must we really', he asked, 'give credit to that oft-repeated assertion that democracy is the kind nurse of genius, and that high literary excellence has flourished with her prime and faded with her decay? Liberty, it is said, is all-powerful to feed the aspirations of high intellects, to hold out hope, and keep alive the flame of mutual rivalry and ambitious struggle for the highest place. Moreover, the prizes which are offered in every free state keep the spirits of her foremost orators whetted by perpetual exercise;[1] they are, as it were, ignited by friction, and naturally blaze forth freely because they are surrounded by freedom. But we of to-day', he continued, 'seem to have learnt in our childhood the lessons of a benignant despotism, to have been cradled in her habits and customs from the time when our minds were still tender, and never to have tasted the fairest and most fruitful fountain of eloquence, I mean liberty. Hence we develop nothing but a fine genius for flattery. This is the reason why, though all other faculties are consistent with the servile condition, no slave ever became an orator; because in him there is a dumb spirit which will not be kept down: his soul is chained: he is like one who has learnt to be ever expecting a blow. For, as Homer says:

'"The day of slavery
Takes half our manly worth away".[2]

As, then (if what I have heard is credible), the cages in

---

[1] Cf. Pericles in Thuc. ii, ἆθλα γὰρ οἶς κεῖται ἀρετῆς μέγιστα τοῖς δὲ καὶ ἄνδρες ἄριστα πολιτεύουσιν.
[2] *Od*. xvii. 322.

which those pygmies commonly called dwarfs are reared
not only stop the growth of the imprisoned creature,
but absolutely make him smaller by compressing every
part of his body, so all despotism, however equitable,
may be defined as a cage of the soul and a general
prison'.

My answer was as follows: 'My dear friend, it is so
easy, and so characteristic of human nature, always to
find fault with the present.[1]   Consider, now, whether the
corruption of genius is to be attributed, not to a world-
wide peace,[2] but rather to the war within us which knows
no limit, which engages all our desires, yes, and still
further to the bad passions which lay siege to us to-day,
and make utter havoc and spoil of our lives.   Are we
not enslaved, nay, are not our careers completely ship-
wrecked, by love of gain, that fever which rages un-
appeased in us all, and love of pleasure?—one the most
debasing, the other the most ignoble of the mind's
diseases.   When I consider it I can find no means by
which we, who hold in such high honour, or, to speak
more correctly, who idolize boundless riches, can close
the door of our souls against those evil spirits which
grow up with them.   For Wealth unmeasured and
unbridled is dogged by Extravagance: she sticks close
to him, and treads in his footsteps: and as soon as he
opens the gates of cities or of houses she enters with him
and makes her abode with him.   And after a time they
build their nests (to use a wise man's words[3]) in that
corner of life, and speedily set about breeding, and beget
Boastfulness, and Vanity, and Wantonness, no base-born
children, but their very own.   And if these also, the

[1] Cf. Byron, 'The good old times—all times when old are
good'.
[2] A euphemism for 'a world-wide tyranny'.
[3] Plato, *Rep*. ix. 573, E.

offspring of Wealth, be allowed to come to their prime, quickly they engender in the soul those pitiless tyrants, Violence, and Lawlessness, and Shamelessness. Whenever a man takes to worshipping what is mortal and irrational[1] in him, and neglects to cherish what is immortal, these are the inevitable results. He never looks up again; he has lost all care for good report; by slow degrees the ruin of his life goes on, until it is consummated all round; all that is great in his soul fades, withers away, and is despised.

'If a judge who passes sentence for a bribe can never more give a free and sound decision on a point of justice or honour (for to him who takes a bribe honour and justice must be measured by his own interests), how can we of to-day expect, when the whole life of each one of us is controlled by bribery, while we lie in wait for other men's death and plan how to get a place in their wills, when we buy gain, from whatever source, each one of us, with our very souls in our slavish greed, how, I say, can we expect, in the midst of such a moral pestilence, that there is still left even one liberal and impartial critic, whose verdict will not be biased by avarice in judging of those great works which live on through all time? Alas! I fear that for such men as we are it is better to serve than to be free. If our appetites were let loose altogether against our neighbours, they would be like wild beasts uncaged, and bring a deluge of calamity on the whole civilized world '.

I ended by remarking generally that the genius of the present age is wasted by that indifference which with a few exceptions runs through the whole of life. If we ever shake off our apathy[2] and apply ourselves to work, it is always with a view to pleasure or applause, not for

---

[1] Reading κἀνόητα.
[2] Cf. Thuc. vi. 26. 2, for this sense of ἀναλαμβάνειν.

that solid advantage which is worthy to be striven for and held in honour.

We had better then leave this generation to its fate, and turn to what follows, which is the subject of the passions, to which we promised early in this treatise to devote a separate work. They play an important part in literature generally, and especially in relation to the Sublime.

APPENDIX TO
DEMETRIUS AND LONGINUS
See page ix

Page 74, line 25: *ērxato de to kakon ex Aithiopias.*

Page 75, line 19: *tōn men peri ta mēdenos axia philo-sophountōn*; line 28: *hēkōn hēmōn eis tēn khōran.*

Page 78, line 13: *men* and *de*; line 31: *dē* and *nu* and *proteron.*

Page 79, line 17: *kai nu ke.*

Page 82, line 1: *Aiakos* and *khiōn*; line 2: *Aiaiē* and *Euios*; line 5: *ēēlios*; line 6: *oreōn*; line 7: *hēlios* and *orōn*; line 11: *panta men ta nea kai kala estin*; line 12: *kalastin*; line 22: *laän anō ōtheske*; line 26: *mē ēpeiros einai*; line 28: *tautēn katoikēoan men Kerkuraioi oikistēs de egeneto*; line 35: *ēōs.*

Page 86, line 18: *sphondulos*; line 19: *ktenes.*

Page 88, line 9: *kinaidiai*; line 14: *autitēs.*

Page 89, line 28: *Aias* and *aien.*

Page 92, line 9: *hēkōn hēmōn eis tēn khōran, pasēs hēmon orthēs ousēs.*

Page 105, lines 1, 2: *Aias . . . bebrōken*; lines 7, 8: *bronta . . . brontē.*

Page 111, lines 19, 20: *panta men ta nea kala estin . . . ēēlios.*

Page 112, line 4: *aiei . . . epibēsomenoisin eïktēn.*

Page 114, lines 8, 9: *laptontes . . . glōssēisi.*

Page 121, line 16: *Trões d' errigēsan, hopōs idon aiolon ophin*; line 21: *Trões d' errigēsan, hopōs ophin aiolon eidon*; lines 25–7: *panta an egrapsen . . . egrapsen an . . . ou paregeneto . . . paregeneto oukhi*; line 29: *de* or *te*; lines 32, 33: *(ētimase de) . . . Skhoinon te Skōlon te.*

Page 122, line 4: *ta hiëra te ta hosia te.*

Page 135, footnote: *philophronestata kai alēthestata.*

Page 136, footnote: *diëphōtisen.*

Page 158, footnote: *eidōlopoiïai.*

Page 160, footnote 4: *hēdusmenōi logōi khōris hekasiōi tōn eidōn.*

Page 165, footnote: *kai pantas tous en huperokhais.*

Page 180, footnote 1: *hupotimēsis.*

Page 182, footnote 2: *ho misōn auton.*

Page 192, lines 6, 7: *touto to psēphisma ton tote tēi polei peristanta kindunon parelthein epoiēsen hōsper nephos*; line 17: *touto to psēphisma hōsper nephos epoiēse ton tote kindunon parelthein*; line 26: *Hōsperei nephos*; footnote 1: *all' eoike maniāi . . . pistis.*

Page 198, footnote 1: *athla gar hois keitai aretēs megista tois de kai andres arista politeuousin.*

Page 200, footnote 1: *kanoēta*; footnote 2: *analambanein.*

INDEX OF AUTHORS AND ARTISTS

referred to in this volume

205